YOUR SERVICE!®

GREAT IDEAS

UP YOUR
SERVICE!

Ron

The Global Service Revolution is an uplifting adventure. What will it take to succeed? More caring, generosity and compassion from everyone, for everyone.

With your help, we can raise the quality of service around the world and *keep it up* for years to come.

Let's make make it happen – together.

GREAT IDEAS

**Tools, tips and proven techniques
to lift your service higher**

Ron Kaufman

www.UpYourService.com

Published by Ron Kaufman Pte Ltd. - 10 9 8 7 6 5 4 3

Ron Kaufman, UP Your Service!, Courseware for Customer Delight, Lift Me Up!, Pick Me Up! and a balloon with the word *"UP"* are all registered trademarks of Ron Kaufman Pte Ltd.

Cover photographs by Tan Teck Hiang.
Cartoons by 'Einstein', Oistein Kristiansen.

The crossword puzzles in this book are provided courtesy of 'Mr. Crossword', Lakhi Sawlani, a specialist in creating customized crossword puzzles. For more information, contact: greatspeeches@yahoo.com

Set in Sabon with Helvetica accents. Printed in Singapore.

UP Your Service! GREAT IDEAS
Tools, tips and proven techniques to lift your service higher
ISBN 981-05-2938-4   268 pages.

1. Customer Service   2. Marketing and Sales   3. Management
4. Self-improvement   5. Ron Kaufman   6. Title

Especially for Customer Service & Training Managers:

Additional copies of this book are available at a discount to support your training programs, service improvement contests and awards, and other special events. For information and fast delivery contact:

Ron Kaufman Pte Ltd
50 Bayshore Park #31-01, Aquamarine Tower, Singapore 469977
Tel: (+65) 6441-2760   Fax: (+65) 6444-8292
e-mail: Ron@RonKaufman.com

Websites: www.RonKaufman.com & www.UpYourService.com

FOREWORD

I have been teaching, traveling and writing about customer service for more than twenty-five years.

All over the world, customers tell me what they like – and don't like – about service in every industry you can imagine.

Managers tell me strategies they use to delight customers, get along with colleagues and build a great service culture.

Service providers share with pride their extra-mile efforts, breakthrough programs and predictably profitable results.

Many of these great ideas appear in my keynote speeches, published articles and training events. Now, the newest collection is here for your full benefit and enjoyment.

Inside you'll find best-practice examples and worst-practice disasters. You'll find insights and updates, tips and techniques, checklists, guidelines, puzzles and more.

Most important, you will find key learning points and actions steps you can use to *improve your service* right away.

Reading this book is smart. Putting what you learn into action is even smarter.

Let's get started!

Ron Kaufman
Singapore, 2005

CONTENTS

CHAPTER 3

Little Things Mean A Lot   **71**

CHAPTER 4

Going the Extra Mile   **95**

CHAPTER 5

People Make the Difference   125

CHAPTER 6

Build Your Service Culture   149

CHAPTER 7
Positive and Powerful Perspectives   **183**

CHAPTER 8
Tools and Tips for Terrific Training   **217**

APPENDIX
Puzzle Answers and Learning Resources 247

CHAPTER

I

STORIES OF
SPECTACULAR SERVICE

True stories of uplifting service inspire people forever.
Create your service legend today!

Do what's desired, not just required

I was staying at a boutique hotel in London and brought a stack of books to the concierge. I asked the young man, 'How much it will cost to ship these books back to my home in Singapore?' He promised to have an answer for me by evening. I left for the day with a smile.

When I returned that afternoon, the concierge handed my books back and said, 'Thirty-two pounds fifty pence'.

I was tired, said 'Thank you', and went up to my room. But I did not smile. And I did not give him a tip.

The next morning I returned to the concierge desk. I was greeted by a very different and somewhat older man. He asked, 'Is there anything I can do to assist you?'

I mentioned the previous day's conversation and asked for directions to the post office. He replied with a question: 'Mr. Kaufman, is this an urgent package?'

'No', I answered. 'I'll be traveling for eight more days in Europe before returning to Singapore.'

'In that case,' he said, 'I'd like to do a bit more research for you. May I do so and give you the results later today?'

I agreed, but I did not smile. And I did not leave a tip.

When I returned in the evening, a two-page letter from the older concierge was waiting in my room. Printed neatly on hotel stationery, it read:

Dear Mr. Kaufman,

Welcome back. I hope you had a good day.

Your books may indeed be sent via the post office for thirty-two pounds fifty pence and will arrive in seven to ten days. The post office is on my way home from the hotel and I would be glad to post them for you tomorrow, if you wish.

Insurance is available at five pounds per hundred valuation and a registered receipt is three pounds. If your books are valuable, I would recommend both.

Should you prefer a more economical route, you may send your package home by sea. The cost is eight pounds twenty-five pence, and delivery takes four to six weeks. However, shipment by sea does not allow for insurance or registered receipt, and if your books are of value, I could not recommend this in good faith.

The post office will make one attempt to deliver your package in Singapore. If you are not home they will leave you a note. You must then visit the post office personally to collect your package.

Given your frequent travel schedule, I understand this may not be convenient for you. Therefore, I have taken the liberty of contacting the international courier services. All feature competitive pricing and can deliver your books within three to four days.

If you are not home, the courier services will leave you a note but then (and here's the difference) they will bring the books *back to your home* at your convenience.

The rate for shipping via courier is forty-two pounds, including a signed receipt and insurance for up to one hundred pounds valuation.

Whichever manner of shipment you choose, your books must be properly packed. We will be glad to do this for you here at the concierge desk.

Mr. Kaufman, I trust this information is helpful to you when making a decision on how to ship your books back to Singapore.

We appreciate that you are staying with us and are grateful for this opportunity to serve you.

Yours faithfully,

The Concierge

PS: If you would like to have your books shipped three or four days hence, thereby assuring you are personally at home to receive them, I can hold the package for you at the concierge desk and ship it on a forward date of your choosing. I can then send you full details of your postal receipt or courier airway bill by e-mail and by fax.

In the morning, I visited the Concierge Desk and gave the older man my instructions. I also gave him a smile.

And a very big tip.

Key Learning Point

There is a big difference between doing what's 'expected' and what's 'appreciated', between answering a question and solving a problem, between completing what's required and doing what's desired.

Action Steps

Look at the range of help, support, ideas and information you give other people during your day. Now find ways to give a little more. How can you be more helpful, proactive, robust, informative, considerate, educational or convenient? How can you make their lives a little easier, faster, smoother, more comfortable or productive? Listen to what other people ask for. Then give them what they want, plus a little more.

Fantastic service? No extra charge!

The extra mile doesn't have to cost an extra dollar for your customer or your company. But going the extra mile can create priceless memories for your customers, goodwill for your company and a fountain of good feelings for you.

At the historic Raffles Hotel in Singapore, each staff member works to delight patrons with many 'memorable experiences'. That phrase is a key element of the mission statement. (It was my privilege to help the Raffles team create it.)

Tourists from around the world come to stay, dine, shop, see – and be seen – at Raffles. Walking the property with cameras in hand, they take photographs they will cherish forever: posing with the stylish doorman, standing in the magnificent lobby, holding hands by the elegant fountain or in the lushly landscaped gardens.

Staff members carefully watch for tourists taking pictures of each other. When they see this 'souvenir photography' in progress, they approach with an offer and a smile. Reaching for the tourist's camera while gesturing toward the attractive background, the staff ask simply, 'May I?'

Tourists understand right away, hand their cameras to the staff and then pose smiling *together* with family and friends.

Click!

A memory is captured. A customer is delighted (and will be delighted again when viewing the pictures back home). Raffles creates goodwill and memories to last a lifetime. What do staff members get? The smiles are their reward.

The doorman's uniform, impeccable lobby, historic fountain and verdant gardens cost a lot of money to maintain. But the memorable moment of service?

It comes at no extra charge.

At One&Only Kanuhura Resort in the Maldives, housekeeping staff watch for young guests traveling with their favorite teddy bears or other stuffed animals.

On the first night, the child's teddy bear is placed high up on the pillows. A chocolate is tucked in its arms.

On the second night, the precious toy is surrounded with beautiful flower blossoms on the table.

On the third night, the beloved bear will be found in an open dresser drawer, holding incense tied with a ribbon.

On the fourth night, the child's cherished friend is found on top of the television, remote control securely in its hands.

On the fifth night, the soft companion is waiting in the bathtub with its arms around a fresh bar of soap.

Each day another playful gesture. It's a wonderful surprise for the children. A pleasure for the parents, too.

One&Only Kanuhura works hard to create 'pleasure beyond your dreams'. That's part of the mission statement. (I was honored to help the Kanuhura team create it.)

The resort itself is a paradise of elegant rooms, romantic restaurants and spectacular spas. These features cost plenty of money to build and maintain. But the memorable moments of service? They come at no extra charge.

Key Learning Point

Going the extra mile can make all the difference between an entirely forgettable interaction and a great service experience. Those extra steps needn't cost a penny. But the rewards can be worth a fortune.

Action Steps

Gather your team for an intensive brainstorming session. Create a long list of things you can do – at no extra cost – to show customers your creativity, care and appreciation. Implement one new idea each month, each week or each day for the rest of the year. It will be the most rewarding year of your life, and the most enjoyable for your customers.

Disneyland makes real magic

We spent two days at Disneyland when my daughter, Brighten, was seven years old. I found the entire park to be a well-oiled, emotionally fulfilling enterprise.

I was impressed by the rides, shows and dedicated staff (called 'cast members').

Many cast members wear colorful pins commemorating Disneyland history and lore: Bambi's birthday, Mickey and his friends, Piglet, Pooh, Beauty and the Beast. On arrival, Brighten was given a lanyard with four identical pins she could *trade* with any cast member in the park.

Each time Brighten met someone with colorful pins she admired, that person knelt down to meet Brighten at eye-level. With a genuine smile, they said enthusiastically, 'Would you like to trade pins with *me*?' It sounded like the most exciting moment of their lives.

At seven years old, choosing can take time, especially with so many pins to pick from. Brighten never felt rushed to make a choice. And every time a trade was made, the staff gave Brighten a big *'Thank you!'* and a friendly smile.

I don't remember which pins Brighten traded. But I will never forget the energy and joy Disneyland staff brought to those precious moments of human contact.

Key Learning Point

Business is not a cold process of swapping services, money and goods. It's a living, thriving appreciation of the dynamic connection between us.

Action Steps

Live today with enthusiasm, energy and joy. You are a chosen cast member in the greatest show on earth – your daily life. (And remember, the curtain is always open.)

Overcoming the nasty pirate

My friend took his son Tommy to Disneyland, hoping for a photograph with Captain Hook. But just as it reached Tommy's turn in line, the photo session ended and Captain Hook stalked off making gruff noises suitable for a pirate.

Little Tommy broke into tears.

Another Disney cast member came along to soothe the boy, gave his parents vouchers for a free dinner in the park and took some additional information.

When they returned to their hotel room that night, a colorful card was waiting on the pillow with a picture of Peter Pan on the front. Inside was a handwritten note:

Dear Tommy, Captain Hook can be quite nasty sometimes. After all, he is a pirate! I hope you enjoy the rest of your stay with all of us at Disneyland.

The card was signed 'Peter Pan', and is cherished today by Tommy (and his parents) more than any old photograph with that nasty Captain Hook!

Key Learning Point

Put positive emotion and a personal touch in your service recovery efforts. Customers will remember and cherish you forever.

Action Steps

The next time something goes wrong for your customer, colleague, friend or family member, make a very special effort to set things right. Be a generous and magical Peter Pan, not a stingy pirate! Take the extra time to do something special, different, memorable and rewarding. You, too, can be someone's new favorite character in the park.

Hold on to the power of your dreams

Disneyland puts on an extravaganza of lights, fireworks, characters, and special effects called 'Fantasmic' every evening.

In the performance, Mickey Mouse has a dream with all his friends singing and dancing with joy.

As my daughter and I watched, suddenly the dream turned into a nightmare, and many evil characters came to life with raging anger, noise and venom. Fire shot from a huge dragon's mouth. Real flames blasted across the water.

Everyone in the audience felt the heat!

At the worst, loudest and most angry moment, when I felt most scared and my daughter was gripping me with both her little hands, Mickey appeared center stage and squeaked loudly: *'Hey! This is MY dream!'*

With a spark from his magic wand he defeated the dragon and blasted the evil characters into submission.

Fear and anger died away, and a huge riverboat steamed around the bend with all the joyful Disney characters on board, waving to the crowd. Fireworks soared and the audience cheered with approval. Brighten shook me with excitement. I cried with appreciation for this magical transformation and life-enhancing performance.

The extravaganza calmed down and the boat sailed away. Fireworks dimmed and all lights shone brightly on Mickey Mouse, high above the crowd. In his most lovable voice he looked out over his customers and friends and said, *'Pretty neat imagination, huh? Ha, ha!'* And with that he was gone, lights out, the show was over. Magic!

Brighten and I hugged in delight.

Disney is so good at moving, making and managing emotions, I didn't even mind the vacuum cleaner they silently attached to my wallet. It was quite full when we went into the park, and altogether empty when we left. Disney runs a magically good business, too!

Key Learning Point

Hey, this is YOUR dream! Whatever fantasies, realities, nightmares or delights you may choose, they are YOURS to change, expand, continue or dissolve. With a zap and a spark of your magical imagination and determination, you can defeat the dastardly demons, and bring your favorite character (the best of you) to life.

Action Steps

When the heat of hard times is scaring you silly, it's time to take a stand for the future. Grab the tools of your life and your magnificent imagination, and say out loud, 'Hey! This is MY dream!'

Then go for it.

Make your life a masterpiece of emotion, affection, appreciation, creativity, generosity, responsibility, enthusiasm and commitment.

Live a life you are proud to lead every day – and are happy to share with others. Live a life that fills you up and turns you on. Make *this* lifetime magic!

Little things can mean a lot

Consumer banks work hard to serve and please their clients. Trouble is, all banks compete on the same 'big things': new products, better interest rates, more branch and ATM locations, 24-hour call centers, easy-to-use websites, convenience, accuracy, speed.

With every bank competing in the same 'big' categories, it can be hard to stand out from the crowd.

One bank found an easy way to achieve a noticeable boost in their customer satisfaction ratings. They discovered something so simple, so small, so 'un-bank-like' their competitors didn't even notice. But customers did.

Here's what the bank understood:

Waiting in line at the bank is a very public place. No matter how quickly the line moves, there is always some time when customers must stand exposed and yet surrounded, inevitably looked over, checked out and sized up by other customers and staff. It can be an awkward time for many.

By the time customers reach the counter, they are usually glad to be served and relieved to be out of the spotlight.

To help set customers at ease, tellers at this bank are trained to 'compliment' each customer quickly as he or she steps up to the counter. Without getting too personal, tellers can choose from a range of simple and polite, yet highly effective comments.

Here are a few statements that work over and over again: 'What a nice smile you have on today', 'That color looks great on you', 'Your handwriting is so easy to read', and the all-time classic for self-conscious men in office attire, 'Nice tie!'

Seems like a tiny thing, doesn't it? Seems like these statements have nothing to do with banking, right?

But these short comments have everything to do with putting people at ease and helping them feel comfortable with themselves – and with others.

By taking care of their customers' spirits as well as their bank accounts, this service-focused bank stands out from the crowd.

Key Learning Point

To be successful with customers you must get the 'big things' right: products, delivery, pricing, processes and people. But sometimes it's the smallest things that make a positive service impression.

Action Steps

Without crossing the bounds of propriety or personal space, what compliments can your staff give to your customers each day?

Attire, preparation, understanding, tone of voice and many other areas can be fertile ground for identifying, recognizing and extending a moment of personal praise. For many people you meet, it may be the only recognition they receive all day.

What a nice thought that this positive moment should come from a great organization like yours, and a great service provider like you.

Give them the 1 percent

I was staying in a small hotel in Tokyo. My seminar would begin early the next morning, and the venue was an hour away.

I called the front desk before going to sleep to order coffee and sliced papaya for 6:30 am. The clerk said Room Service only opened at 7:30 am. Too late for comfort.

I thought coffee and papaya could be easily prepared by the first person into the kitchen and asked hopefully, 'How about delivery at 7:00 am?'

'Ah, 7:00 am', the receptionist sighed in careful English. 'I can tell you now it is 99 percent difficult.'

'Thank you,' I replied. 'Please give me the 1 percent.'

He laughed over the phone and said, 'I understand.' And then he wished me goodnight.

At 7:00 am the doorbell rang. Room Service appeared with hot coffee and sliced papaya. The 1 percent had delivered.

Key Learning Point

Everyone has rules to follow, schedules, systems and procedures. Close to those plans is a border where flexibility can be applied – even if it's only 1 percent. One percent can make all the difference.

The next time your customer asks for something extra or something different, needs a little more care, compassion or effort, you can tell them it is '99 percent difficult' – or you can deliver the 1 percent.

Action Steps

Look carefully at the rules and procedures you follow every day. Now look again to see what can be changed or adapted when required. Of course some rules should never be broken: safety, security, integrity, legal compliance and health. But when you *can* be flexible, perhaps you *should*. Some rules are meant to be bent.

Three steps to welcome

What a conversation! A British gentleman working in global logistics, his American entertainer wife who recently became a mother, an Australian event coordinator and me. Four different cultures – and different points of view.

We talked about the service we received at retail stores, banks, restaurants, hotels and airlines around the world. We each had very different opinions about what constitutes 'good service'.

The logistics guy likes fast and efficient; pleasantries are incidental. The entertainer wants time to browse before she is approached, and feels 'hurried' if someone comes too close, too soon. The Australian feels just the opposite. She wants attention right away or she walks right out the door. And me? I like the 'human touch': a smile, friendly tone of voice, a twinkle in the eye.

Our differences are not surprising given our backgrounds. But what a challenge for committed service providers!

Should your service be reserved and polite, or outgoing and friendly? Should you be fast and efficient, or personal and attentive? Should you initiate contact and offer immediate help, or wait discreetly until you are asked?

What pleases one customer may easily disturb another. But you've got to do something. So what should you do?

Beneath the preferences of one person and another, I found

'Three Steps to Welcome' that *always* apply:

1. Acknowledge the person
2. Make a positive gesture
3. Extend an offer to help

Acknowledge the person means letting *them* know that *you* know they are there. This can be done with simple eye contact, a tip of your head or a momentary opening of your hand.

Have you ever been in a store with sales staff who completely ignored you? Did you feel awkward as they talked on the phone, or invisible as they chatted with each other?

Have you ever been happy to wait several minutes while a clerk helped someone else, because she acknowledged you first with a tiny gesture, raised eyebrows or a smile?

It doesn't take much to acknowledge another person. But it *does* require something. One small gesture makes the difference.

Make a positive gesture doesn't mean waving your hands and shouting 'C'mon in!' That might be good for a carnival or a bustling street on a busy night. But theatrics can be out of place at government offices, hospitals or jewelry stores where couples search slowly for rings.

At the government service counter, a positive gesture could be simply, 'Next, please'. In a museum or fine restaurant, a slight tilt from the waist is enough. In a retail store, the wide sweep of your hand invites shoppers to browse freely.

Extend an offer to help is easy when spoken: 'How may I help you?' 'Your passport, please', 'Good morning. My name is Ron'. In silence, two open hands mean 'I am here to help you'. One guiding palm says 'Come this way', or 'Have a seat'.

Your 'Three Steps to Welcome' will depend on where you work, whom you serve and what reputation you wish to create. This may take fine-tuning before you get it right.

When Giordano clothing stores first opened, the staff were too excited, cheering new customers and scaring timid ones right out of the store! Today, Giordano's has refined the welcoming process to an elegant dance of body language, gestures, facial expressions and spoken words. They watch customers carefully and observe how they react. Staff know when to go slow and let new shoppers browse, and when to step forward with personal attention.

American Express went too far with their initial Platinum Card telephone service. Caller ID allowed Amex to know who was calling and answer the phone using the customer's name. But customers were shocked to be addressed by name before they had introduced themselves. (Now Amex only uses your name after you've said it once yourself.)

Raffles Hotel understands that too much service can become unpleasant service. A personal welcome by the chef, the manager, the hostess, every waiter and busboy will scuttle the best hospitality intentions at dinner. Raffles' Chief Executive Officer likens their style of service to 'a gentle breeze', soothing you when you want it, but never blowing too hard in your face.

Key Learning Point

Everyone entering your place of work should receive acknowledgment, positive gestures and an appropriate offer of assistance.

Action Steps

Survey customers of all types: old and young, male and female, hurried and relaxed, on a budget or on a spree. Ask them how they like to be greeted. What would be 'too much', what would be 'too little'?

Discuss the results with your colleagues and ask their opinions, too.

Decide which 'Three Steps to Welcome' match your company's image and your customer base. Then set standards, practice with role-plays, train and supervise new staff. Use these three steps to make *your* customers feel recognized, appreciated and welcome.

Service is a two-way street

Hi Ron,

I was having trouble with a set of tires I purchased for my automobile. The ride was rough and unacceptable. The store was willing to exchange the tires or give me a refund. However, it was not definite that the tires were actually the cause of my problem.

Paul, the mechanic servicing my cars for the last six years, offered to take a look. His son Mike did a diagnostic check that took an hour and a half. Afterwards, they explained what the real problem was. Then they offered a recommendation and I followed their advice. The problem was resolved with an exchange of tires to a different model.

This service from Paul and Mike is excellent customer care. But it gets even better. Paul refused to accept any payment from me for the diagnostic service performed on my automobile. And it gets even better than that! Five days later I received a 'Thank You!' card from them both. They thanked me for letting them serve me even though they didn't charge anything after discovering the cause of my problem. Now *that* is great customer service!

I turned around and thanked them and their crew by having pizza sent over to their repair shop for lunch. The entire experience was truly delicious 'food for thought'.

Mel S., Motorola

           *   *   *

Dear Mel,

Bravo to you and to your mechanics. This story illustrates three key principles in service.

First, Paul and Mike understand the 'lifetime value of a customer'. You have been bringing your car to their shop for six years. You have likely spent thousands of dollars with them during this time. They can *afford* to give you an hour or two of diagnostic service at no charge. And with a gesture of generosity like that, you will spend thousands more with them in the years to come.

Second, the card they sent you was a brilliant investment of time and effort. Writing the card took no more than five minutes – yet it created an emotional impact no amount of paid advertising will ever match. Your 'positive word-of-mouth' when telling this story to others will be more credible than any newspaper advertising, more lasting than any radio or television commercial. Great service providers, Paul and Mike. (Smart business people, too.)

Third, your action in sending a pizza and sharing your story with me demonstrates that great service really is a two-way street. What you send out comes back. What goes around, comes around. When you give with a generous spirit and an open heart, the world brings great things back to you.

Wishing you all the best, Mel. May you continue to enjoy smooth rides and smooth service.

Key Learning Point

Delivering superior service isn't rocket science. The fundamentals of world-class service are easy to learn – but not always easy to apply. What makes one service provider better than another is not more theory or information. It's more action!

Action Steps

Choose one of the fundamental service principles in this book and put it into action this week. It doesn't matter which principle you choose. They all work well – when you do.

How to be a better customer

When you give better service, your customers will appreciate you more. But when you give lousy service, your customers can be a pain in the neck.

The flip side is also true. If you are an appreciative and considerate customer, service providers will tend to serve you better. If you rant and rave and pound the table, people serve you grudgingly, if at all.

Great training programs (like 'UP Your Service College'®) can help create better customer service providers. But there's little training on how you can be a better customer!

Here's a list of tips I use to be a better customer and to enjoy receiving better service:

1. Always be appreciative and polite. Remember, there is a fellow human being on the other end of your telephone call, e-mail message or just across the counter. I begin the service interaction with a quick comment: 'Hi. Thank you for helping me. I really appreciate it.' (This takes about two seconds.)

2. Get the service provider's name, and then use it. I make it short and friendly by asking, 'Who am I speaking with please?' or if we are face-to-face, simply 'May I know your name?' Once they tell me, I repeat it with a smile on my face and in my voice. 'Hello (name here). My name is Ron.' This creates a personal connection. (It takes about four seconds.)

3. Be 'UP' in your own energy (if you can). Many service providers face customer after customer...all day long. The routine can be a drag. When one customer appears with a genuine smile and positive energy to spare, he or she stands out for special care and treatment. You can be that special customer. Let your enthusiasm be contagious.

4. Give your details the way your service provider asks for them. Every service professional has a preferred way of gathering data that fits their forms, computer screen or procedures. Have all your information ready to go, but give it in the order he or she prefers.

   Simply say, 'I have my name, customer number, invoice number, telephone, address and product details ready. Which would you like first?' This lets the service provider know you are prepared and efficient to work with. They appreciate that and can show their appreciation through better service rendered to you. (The time you take getting everything in order will save you even more time once you are in the service conversation.)

5. Check each step along the way. Simply repeat or paraphrase what the service provider states or promises to do. This allows you to progress together step-by-step through the service process and catch any questions or misunderstandings early on. Small changes can be made quickly and more easily as you go along, than if you wait until everything has been concluded.

6. Confirm next steps. Be sure you understand what will happen next: what they will do, what you should do and what you can both expect from each other. Confirm dates, times, amounts, promises, responsibilities and obligations. Write down whatever you agree on, and ask that a confirmation be sent to you by e-mail, hard copy or fax. When the confirmation arrives, check it carefully to ensure everything is written as agreed.

7. If appropriate, commiserate with the service provider. Some people can't help letting their frustration show. They may be upset by a previous customer or by some aspect of their work: a slow computer, high call volume, overwhelming response, pressure from managers or even personal events at home.

   When you hear a word or tone of upset from your service provider, be the one to soothe them. I simply say, 'Sorry to hear things are a bit frustrating for you', and then I repeat, 'I really appreciate your help.' This is so powerful! After empathizing with their frustration, I've had service providers go an extra hundred miles to ensure *my* service experience had no frustration at all.

8. Finally, show real appreciation. A warm 'thank you' over the phone or in person is always appropriate. If your service provider deserves more, give more. A nicely written compliment to the organization can make a huge difference in someone's day, or in their career.

And who knows? The one you praise may serve you again another day with the same pleasure, efficiency and delight.

Key Learning Point

Service is a two-way street. The traffic of goodwill flows equally between customers and service providers. Don't wait for someone else to make your day. Be the customer who shines with preparation and appreciation. The service you receive will be the reward you deserve.

Action Steps

The next time you need service, bring the best of yourself to the interaction. If you want good things to come to you, start the ball rolling by extending goodwill to others.

Puzzle this: How spectacular is your service?

Answers in the Appendix...but try working them out first!

Puzzle clues

Across

1   Seek to obtain
2   The kind of service you strive *never* to provide
3   Assessment reports
7   Section of an organization
10 Peruse or recite
11 The emotion we hope our customers feel
12 High service level results in a ____ increase in sales
15 Often better at managing a country than a business
16 Service in a hurry
18 What well-trained employees are
19 Sample, savor
20 Different from the previous one
21 Most recent
23 The foresight necessary for a business to succeed
24 Small gift of money in appreciation of service
25 Word used to question reason or purpose

Down

1   Customers are loyal when we ____ more value
2   To UP your service, raise this limit higher
4   Authenticity
5   Hunger for praise and appreciation
6   Listening carefully to customers makes relation-
    ships more ____
8   Give money in return for a service
9   The number of times *not* to make the same mistake
13 Customer service staff should be empowered to
    show this
14 Annoyed
15 This must prevail in any argument (two words)
17 To resolve disputes satisfactorily
18 Seller
22 Be higher or better than

CHAPTER

2

ADDING SERVICE VALUE

Customers get value in so many ways.
Do everything you can do to add more!

Connect *to* your customers *through* your customers

We all live and work in a constellation of relationships based on service. You can see this with the customers you serve and the suppliers who serve you. But this is also true with colleagues, employees, managers, family, friends, government agencies and community members.

When you improve service in every direction of your life, you'll find new ways to connect to your customers, through your customers.

Paul in South Africa explains:

'Passing on supplier benefits to our customers' employees creates a deep-rooted loyalty that is hard to break. We supply fuel to a company with a large fleet of trucks on commercial contract. But we also give the truck drivers a special deal on fuel for their personal cars and on any purchases they make at our convenience stores. This creates brand familiarity and appreciation that are part of their daily lives.'

What a positive and productive idea. But how many suppliers are doing this? Are yours? Are you?

Here's another example:

Sandy and Savvy enjoy vacations at The Wickaninnish Inn in Tofino, Canada. The hotel knows they adore their friendly dog, Tess, and bring her along whenever they visit. Two weeks before a recent vacation, *the dog* received this letter:

> Dear Tess,
>
> It was good to learn you will be bringing your parents to the Wickaninnish Inn. Upon arrival at the Inn there will be some paperwork for one of your

parents to complete regarding responsibility for you while at the Inn. Once that is complete and you are settled in your room, the 1.5 mile long Chesterman Beach awaits, and there are many sticks for you to choose from!

Do remember not to chase the birds, as many of them use the beach as a resting and feeding area on their migration route. There is a washing station and towel storage as you leave the beach, where you can rinse off salt water or sandy paws and dry off.

Please be aware that the District of Tofino requires all dogs to be on a leash at all times. This bylaw does include all public beaches including Chesterman Beach. Remind your parents to bring your leash!

A few final points to remember are that we ask you to wear your leash at all times in the common areas of the Inn, and that you never be left unattended in the room unless you have brought your portable house. We do have a couple of houses available at the Inn. Lastly, your parents are paying an additional $20.00 per night for your stay, so treat them kindly and do not make off with their slippers.

We look forward to seeing you at the Inn.

Sincerely,

Crystal @ The Wickaninnish Inn

What a smart letter!

The Wickaninnish Inn serves the 'paying' customer by writing to the 'pawing' customer with all the rules and regulations. Everything is clearly stated, but no one takes offense. In fact, I'll bet Tess's tail is wagging (Sandy's and Savvy's, too).

Here's another powerful example: The Prisons Department in Singapore says: 'Our mission in life is to get criminals out of prison.'

To help prisoners *rehab*, *renew, restart* and *not return*, the department manages a holistic program of in-care and after-care service. The Prisons Department connects *to* each ex-offender by connecting *through* the police, courts, family members, friends, neighbors, volunteers, employers and society at large.

Question: Who is the customer?

Answer: Everyone.

Key Learning Point

Connecting with your customers can include much more than just direct contact. The people in your customers' lives could be people you serve, too.

Action Steps

Draw a bicycle wheel with your customers in the center. Put key people (and pets!) in your customers' lives on each of the connecting spokes.

Now find new ways to serve those 'connected people' better. Ask them what you might do to help, add value or simply make things easier. Check with your customers, too. Remember, each time you connect *through* your customers, you also connect *to* your customers.

How to stand out from the crowd

In today's competitive markets, smart companies strive to 'stand out' from others in the crowd. Low pricing is one approach, but it eats away your profit margin. Super-high quality is another approach, but can be hard to deliver if your product is a commodity item, easily available from other sources or vendors.

Fabulous service can help a great deal – and it can be done in so many ways!

Here's one approach that delights me from a web-based CD store with an attitude of customer adoration. Read the cheeky message I received recently, and see if it doesn't make you smile, too.

Dear Ron,

Thanks for your order with CD Baby!

Your CD has been gently taken from our CD Baby shelves with sterilized, contamination-free gloves and placed onto a satin pillow.

A team of 50 devoted employees inspected your CD and polished it to make sure it was in the best possible condition before mailing.

Our packing specialist from Japan lit a candle, and a hush fell over the crowd as he put your CD into the finest gold-lined box that money can buy.

We all had a wonderful celebration afterwards and the whole party marched down the street to the post office, where the entire town of Portland waved 'Bon Voyage!' to your package, on its way to you in our private CD Baby luxury jet.

I hope you had a wonderful time shopping at CD Baby. We sure had a wonderful time taking care of you. Your picture is on our wall as 'Customer of the Year'. We're all exhausted, but can't wait for you to come back to CDBABY.COM!

Thank you once again,

Derek Sivers, President
CD Baby, the little CD store with the best new independent music, http://www.cdbaby.com

I had such a great time reading this note and sharing it here with you.

Key Learning Point

To stand out from the crowd, find a style you like and take it to a whole new level. Consider the wisdom in this magnificent quote (I live my life in part on its guidance): *'Be outrageous. It's the only place that isn't crowded!'*

Action Steps

Decide what you want to be known for and find a way to do it, be it, say it, give it, live it and share it more outrageously than ever before.

Go ahead and shoot for the moon. Even if you miss, you'll still be among the stars.

Break the law, get good service

Mary works at the Judicial Branch of the Centralized Infractions Bureau of a major metropolitan area. She enjoys giving her 'customers' good service – and is always looking for ways to improve.

'However,' she explained, 'the problem we face is quite obvious. Being a government enforcement agency, we must follow many rules and there is literally zero leeway in the options we can give defendants in how to take care of their infractions.'

Mary is absolutely right.

Many enforcement and regulatory agencies face similar 'customer service' situations: police departments, judicial courts, customs offices, immigration counters and licensing bureaus, to name a few. Staff may be eager to provide wonderful service, but they cannot jeopardize the integrity of the law or equality in the administration of justice.

Can these government officers be flexible and change the rules? No, that would make a mockery of the law.

Can they give highly personalized and customized service? No, that could lead to allegations of favoritism, partiality and scandal.

But can government departments and civil servants offer speed? Yes. Courtesy? Yes. Useful and easy-to-understand information? Yes. Proactive advice on what to expect and how to navigate each step in the process? Yes. On-line applications and filing systems? Yes. Convenient locations? Yes. Extended hours of operation? Yes. An attractive physical environment? Yes. Support materials such as pens, paper, photocopy machines and telephones? Yes. Dignity and respect for all?

Yes, yes, yes!

I call these different aspects of service your 'value dimensions'. There are many 'value dimensions' that apply in every service situation, even in the judicial system.

No matter who you are, what you do or where you work, you can find a way to increase service value and make your service better.

Key Learning Point

Every interactive situation offers an opportunity to improve your service to others. If you can't be flexible, be fast. If you can't be generous, be courteous. If you can't be personal, be informative. If you can't be low price, be high value.

Never let your situation become an excuse for giving up. Find another way to serve someone better.

Action Steps

Stop whining, complaining or using circumstances as an excuse for not improving your service. Everyone can make service improvements, no matter who you are or where you are. Look around. Find a better way. Then do it.

PS: Don't use this lesson to avoid making service improvements where you can and should. If you *can* be flexible, bend. If you *can* be generous, give. If you *can* be faster, hustle.

In your best interest

A diversified medical group suffered from a common procedure that frustrated patients, doctors and laboratory technicians every day.

First, doctors sent their patients to the laboratory for tests. After the tests, patients asked the laboratory technicians for results.

When technicians shared the test results, patients often got upset. When patients got upset, doctors got upset. Doctors preferred to explain test results to their patients personally and offer next steps for treatment.

But if technicians did not give patients their test results immediately, patients complained that information was being withheld and claimed the laboratory technicians were unhelpful.

The situation was clearly lose-lose-lose: patients, doctors and laboratory technicians – everyone got upset.

(Does this ever happen in your organization? Do your customers ever become frustrated, angry or confused? Do your staff get upset when your customers are upset? Does your brand image suffer, too? Are there 'lose-lose-lose' situations lurking in your business?)

The medical group asked me for help. I diagnosed the situation as a case of 'unmanaged customer expectations'. If you were a patient, wouldn't you want to know your test results right away?

If you were a doctor, wouldn't you be upset if your patient knew the results before you did? If you were a technician, wouldn't you feel caught in the middle?

We solved this problem with a simple but powerful system called 'In Your Best Interest'.

When doctors order lab tests, they use a printed checklist to indicate which procedures are required. At the top of the checklist, in bold letters, is now printed this statement:

> 'IN YOUR BEST INTEREST, all laboratory results will be sent to your doctor who will explain them to you personally and discuss the most appropriate treatment.'

Many doctors now read this statement to their patients. Many patients read the statement themselves. Most patients understand the message, but many are so nervous about their upcoming tests, they don't pay attention.

In the waiting room of the laboratory, a large poster now hangs on the wall. In bold letters the poster reads:

> 'IN YOUR BEST INTEREST, all laboratory results will be sent to your doctor who will explain them to you personally and discuss the most appropriate treatment.'

All patients can see the sign, and many understand the message. But some are so anxious about their upcoming tests, they still don't pay attention.

After the tests are done, a small percentage of patients *still* ask laboratory technicians for an immediate explanation of the results. For those few, the lab technicians have been trained to say one simple sentence in a compassionate and caring manner:

> 'IN YOUR BEST INTEREST, all laboratory results will be sent to your doctor who will explain them to you personally and discuss the most appropriate treatment.'

By this time, everyone pays attention. Patients wait to see their doctors. Doctors can fully inform their patients. And laboratory technicians can do their job compassionately without getting caught in the middle.

That's a 'win-win-win' for everyone.

Key Learning Point

Customers may become confused or frustrated by your policies and procedures. This is especially common in large organizations. But it's not productive to blame your customers or your colleagues – that only makes things worse.

What *is* effective is to resolve the situation permanently by improving the clarity and consistency of your communications.

Action Steps

Find a point of friction where your customers or colleagues get upset. Choose a tension point that has persisted for many months. Do people complain about your applications and procedures? Are your policies hard to understand? Is your guarantee confusing? Have your systems grown slowly out-of-date?

There may be good reasons why your policies and procedures were created. But the explanation may be missing today or the reason may no longer apply. In either case, you can improve the situation dramatically by enhancing your communications, streamlining the procedure or changing the policy itself.

It makes good sense to fix whatever you can, whenever you can. After all, 'win-win-win' is also *in your best interest.*

To be distinctive, be different

There are many ways for a business to 'stand out from the crowd'. One approach is to give your customers more of what they ask for. If others are fast, you go faster. If others are clean, you be cleaner. If others are cheap, you can discount deeper. If your competitors offer a lot, you offer even more.

This approach has obvious problems. First, your top position can be overtaken by anyone else offering 'even more'. Second, the cost of escalation can become overwhelming. You need happy customers but healthy profits, too.

A different approach is worth your time and effort: Find completely new and different ways to surprise, intrigue, support, nurture and delight your customers.

For example, international airlines compete on big seats, quality service, good wine and movies. But Virgin Atlantic was first to offer neck and shoulder massages on all long-distance flights. They stand out in the airline crowd.

Most quick-service restaurants provide clean counters, fast delivery and low prices. But McDonald's put enormous, colorful slides for children inside their restaurant buildings. McDonald's french fries are made from potatoes, much like everyone else's. Their play space stands out in the fast-food crowd.

How many times have you left your tube of toothpaste wet, wrinkled and gooey on the bathroom sink? Procter & Gamble helped solve the problem with the first standup toothpaste tube. Their toothpaste container stands out from the crowd.

The Garden Café in Dubai serves many customers who

are bachelors, always on the move and short of time. So the Café provides a lunch and dinner buffet of good food and drinks, but also irons your shirts and shines your shoes while you eat!

You can do this, too. (Stand out from the crowd, not the laundry.)

Key Learning Point

Anyone can compete by doing 'more' of what's already expected. But there's another way to be distinctive: Be different!

Action Steps

Make a list of all the 'usual ways' your organization offers good customer service. Now think of totally different ways you could surprise, intrigue or delight.

What bothers your customers? How can you fix it? What do they do before or after your service? How can you integrate it? What do they bring, carry or take away? How can you replace it?

The first bookstore to offer plush chairs and fresh coffee changed the industry completely. The first bank that offered drive-through service transformed our expectations. What can YOU do to stand out, stand up – be different?

Create convenience for the customer

If you travel by air, you know how stringent security can be in airports around the world. Many items previously allowed onboard are now banned, confiscated and, in many cases, discarded by security personnel.

Losing a nail file or a pair of scissors may not seem like much, but hairdressers pay a lot for professional scissors; a letter opener may be a sentimental gift from a friend; a pocket knife could be an heirloom handed down from grandfather to father to son.

What can be done to keep these items out of the aircraft cabin, but safely delivered back to the owner?

Some airlines will put the offending item in a small pouch, store it in the aircraft's baggage hold, and give it back to the passenger at the destination. But this service takes precious time before departure, and some airports simply don't allow it. As a customer you have only two choices: give up the item forever, or give up your seat on the flight.

Allan in Australia proposed another solution. He suggests:

'Many airline customers have become confused about which articles may be detected and rejected by security as they board domestic and international aircraft.

'My suggestion is to set up automated self-service mailboxes near security screening that can dispense stamped, padded envelopes. If an article such as a penknife or nail file is rejected, the traveler can go immediately to the mailbox and quickly:

1. weigh the item and indicate the destination country,

2. place sufficient money in the machine (or use a credit card),

3. receive a stamped, padded, self-sealing envelope,

4. address it to themselves at their destination,

5. drop it in the mailbox, and

6. get back to the gate in plenty of time for their flight.

'The franchise for these mailboxes could be sold to book-
stores or coffee shop proprietors at each airport. This
would help security resolve the distress innocent travelers suffer when they must surrender personal items of
great sentimental value.

'Many airports have post offices, but they are rarely
close to security, and never open 24 hours – and we all
know about slow-moving lines at security screening.'

By focusing on customer concerns, Allan came up with an
idea that is quick, easy, practical, cost-effective, reduces
hassles for everyone, requires no additional labor and opens
up a new avenue for revenue and compliments from very
appreciative customers.

Key Learning Point

Customers are emotional creatures and may have concerns not addressed by your focus on speed, accuracy, price, security, size, weight
or location. Helping customers comply with procedures is important.
But helping them feel good about their compliance is very important,
too. Find ways to do both and you'll gain your customers' appreciation,
recognition and respect.

Action Steps

Put yourself in your customers' shoes. What's the greatest inconvenience customers must endure when doing business with you? What
can you do to make that process more convenient, flexible, personal or
attractive? How can you anticipate and help them avoid the hassle? If
they must comply, how can you recognize, praise or congratulate them
for getting it done?

Being a customer is not always easy. At your place of business, make it
as painless and rewarding as you can.

Make things easy for your customer

I have three complaints and three suggestions.

One: I am sick and tired of struggling with badly designed order forms that ask me to write my credit card number in tiny little boxes.

Two: I'm tired of getting forms from companies asking me to provide information the company already has.

Three: I'm fed up with firms that say, 'For more information visit our website', without giving me the specific URL that takes me directly to the page I need.

It's time for every company and every worker to wake up and realize that making things easy for your customers is a winning strategy in business (and in life).

Here are some tactics that will help:

One: Review every point of contact your customer encounters. Ask yourself, 'How can we make this easier, more pleasurable or more convenient?' When you find something that can be improved, do it.

Two: Any time you want your customer to apply, renew, order or confirm anything, do everything you can to pre-fill the appropriate information. If you already know their address, put it on the form. If you already have their serial number, print it on the card. If you already have their account information, put it in the appropriate boxes, fields or spaces.

Three: When you refer customers to your website, send them to the exact page whenever you can. Taking a moment to provide the correct URL shows respect for their time and increases the likelihood they will actually click through and find what they seek.

For example, to read chapters from my other books, visit: http://www.RonKaufman.com/products.html

For an online interview with questions and answers, visit: http://www.RonKaufman.com/media/interviewa.html

For free audio and video clips featuring stories and examples, visit: http://www.RonKaufman.com/videos.html

Key Learning Point

Making things easy for your customers makes good business sense. At Amazon.com I can order a book with literally just *one click*. How? They already have my address, shipping preference and credit card information from my past orders. With ordering so easy, I am a very regular – and profitable – customer.

Action Steps

What is *your* version of Amazon's 'one click'? To find out, test all current systems from your customers' point of view. Keep track of every step your customers must take to get what they want and accomplish what they need. Then form a team whose mission is to make your procedures smoother, faster, easier, more accurate and trouble-free. Keep working until you can remove a step or two – or six. Your customers will appreciate and reward you.

Listen to the language

I called an electronics company last week to arrange repair of our television. The automated answering system offered these three options:

For Sales, press 1.

For Technical Support, press 2.

For the Office of Customer Delight, press 3.

I pressed 3 and was connected to a service professional who quickly took care of my needs.

What surprised me was not the polite efficiency of the staff, but the name of menu option 3!

Listen to this evolution (in many industries it's happened quietly over several years): the Product Repair Center became the Product Service Center which became the Customer Service Center which was renamed the Customer Care Center which is now called the Office of Customer Delight.

Can you hear the difference? Of course you can. Language makes a difference!

What do you call the departments in your organization? The Office of Credit Control sounds quite different than The Department for Credit Approval. The financial criteria may be exactly the same, but the underlying attitude toward your customers is not.

Position titles also matter. Sales Manager is a common title, but how many customers want to be 'sold'? Business Development Manager might be better, but business development is your company's concern, not necessarily your customer's.

So what *should* you call that important job of closing sales and making deals? Guarantor of Client Success? Bold Champion for Customer Value? Supreme Supervisor of Spectacular Service?

How creative can you, or should you, try to be?

Key Learning Point

Department names and position titles send clear messages to your customers and your staff. Make sure your company language promotes success and a customer-friendly point of view. Remember, language makes a difference!

Action Steps

Review the names of all offices, positions and departments in your organization. What point of view is embodied in each? If your terms are industry jargon, internally focused, customer unfriendly or simply out-of-date, it's time to make a change.

Note: This approach makes sense for people who have contact with external customers, not necessarily for those who work deep inside highly technical organizations.

For example, the person whose business card reads: 'Technical Software Specialist, XE73 Packet Switch' should probably be called just that!

Which way do I go?

Dubai International Airport is one of my favorite airports in the world. It's big, clean and exciting. But in such a terrific environment, little inconveniences stand out.

Inside this great airport is a modern and attractive hotel. Inside the transit area is an elevator going up from arrivals and departures to the hotel floors.

In the elevator, clear buttons read: Departures, Arrivals, Hotel 1, and Hotel 2.

If you wanted to check-in at the hotel, which button would you push?

We pushed 'Hotel 1', which took us to a residential floor with no reception desk; only a long hallway with locked hotel room doors.

We got back in the elevator and pushed 'Hotel 2', which took us up to another floor with a long hallway of locked doors.

We got back in the elevator and wondered where to go. Thinking we must have missed something, we returned to the departure level.

Once again, however, there was nothing and no one to assist us. Finally, with only one choice left, we got back in the elevator and pressed 'Arrivals'.

Stepping out of the elevator we turned left and walked toward a bar in a large lobby area. It was early afternoon and no one was behind the counter.

We turned around and saw another counter across the lobby. There was no sign, but there were two people waving at us and smiling.

We crossed the landing and found ourselves, finally, at the hotel reception counter.

When I explained what happened in the elevator, the staff apologized and said, 'We know. It happens all the time.'

I asked why there was no sign in the elevator pointing to the hotel reception desk. I asked why there was no sign outside the elevator directing guests to 'Reception'. I asked why there was no sign even at the desk itself.

'We know,' she said again politely. 'Everyone asks us that. We have asked for signs many times, but we are still waiting. The airport did a renovation behind the desk recently to change the colors, and we were hoping for signs, but they did not come.'

On my way out, we took a different elevator. Someone (in desperation?) had made a small sign reading 'Reception' and pasted it inside the elevator near the buttons. The little sign is paper, handmade and peeling.

The handwritten sign looks pathetic amid such elegant steel and glass, but at least in one elevator someone did something – and that's better than doing nothing at all.

Key Learning Point

Awkward service situations can persist for days, months, even years, with no one looking carefully to improve them. Is this happening at your company or organization?

If you look closely, can you find a 'small thing' that could be done better? Will you make that change right now or will you allow another day, month or year of customer inconvenience to pass ?

Action Steps

I always recommend improvements when I see the opportunity and the need. You can do this, too. But remember, *action* counts. Just talking about it doesn't count for much.

PS: One week after I sent this suggestion to the airport, new elevator signage was installed. Bravo Dubai Airport!

Can you read your name?

Dubai Airport also has an official greeting service for arriving passengers called 'Marhaba'.

Marhaba is staffed with attractively dressed men and women who meet designated passengers and then escort them through immigration and customs.

Marhaba prints long lists of individuals who are scheduled to receive this special welcome service. These lists are located at the bottom of an escalator, just at the point where travelers must step off with their carry-on bags and move quickly away from the crush of passengers descending behind them.

At that very point, where time is short and attention is already diverted, Marhaba places a sign full of names, printed in THICK, BLACK, BLOCK CAPITAL letters with hardly any space at all between them.

The names are difficult to read when one is standing still, and almost impossible when the escalator is moving.

If you know Marhaba service has been arranged for you, then you must pause to reconfirm.

If you are not sure, or don't know what the sign is about, you also pause. This results in a gaggle of people stopping, pausing, looking and wondering in front of a sign that is hard to read, at a critical point in the flow of passengers through one of the best airports in the world.

A change in the lettering style would be so simple to do. By using an upper and lower case serif font (like you are reading in this book), passengers could more easily read the signs and quickly see their names.

I have offered this suggestion several times to the friendly Marhaba staff. Each time they agree it would be a good idea, but then smile and say, 'It's always been like that.' (That's a bad reason not to make a good improvement.)

Key Learning Point

The big things count in business and in life: quality products, fast delivery, friendly and competent staff. But little things count, too. And little things can make a big difference for your customer.

Action Steps

Ask your frontline staff what 'little things' upset your customers. What 'silly questions' do customers ask day after day? What complaints do your staff hear over and over again? What causes your customers frustration, confusion and anger? Find it. Then fix it.

PS: Two months after I sent this suggestion to the airport, the signage was exactly the same....

This call requires someone else. Now what?

Kumarie asked about a common service situation:

'Sometimes we handle calls on behalf of others when they are not around. Occasionally we can only help to a certain extent. If the query gets deeper than we can handle, we say "Sorry but I am only answering on behalf of so and so," or "I am covering the duty of someone else who is really the right person to help you."

'I'm afraid this message may sound bad to our customers who might think, "Are you saying I should stop asking you anything further? Should I wait for the person in charge to come back? Have you been wasting my time?"

'Your comments and advice, please.'

Great question, Kumarie! Here is my reply:

It is always good to offer help. It's also important to be honest if you are not the very best person to answer the question. When this is the case, tell your customer you will do everything you can to assist, and that you will forward their question to your colleague if necessary.

Throughout the call, take notes of all information given by your customer. If it becomes clear that you must refer them to someone else, explain honestly and calmly as follows:

'Mr. Customer, this question is now at a point where I want to be sure we get exactly the right answer for you. To do this properly, allow me to bring this matter to my colleague Ms. 123, who is the right person to help us resolve this matter and find the information you need.

'I have taken careful notes throughout our conversation and will share this information with Ms. 123 as soon as she returns. It will take me XX minutes/hours to review this with her, after which I will call you back personally, or make sure Ms. 123 calls you back with the information you need.

'In the meantime, let me give you the spelling of my name and direct phone line, so that you are able to easily call me again if you have any further questions.'

Note the following key points in my reply:

1. You retain primary responsibility for your caller's satisfaction. You are not passing the buck, dropping the ball or letting a customer fall through the cracks.

2. You prepare your customer early for the possibility that you may be unable to complete the service required. You anticipate the need for referral to a colleague by a) explaining upfront that you will make every effort to help, b) letting the customer know there are others who will help if needed, and c) taking notes throughout the process to facilitate referral to your colleague if required.

3. You pride yourself in 'closing the loop' personally, either by calling back, or making sure someone else does, and by giving your personal contact information.

   If you follow this carefully planned route, your customer's satisfaction will climb higher, even if you are unable to personally answer their question.

I hope this helps, and thank you again for asking.

Key Learning Point

Once customers make contact with someone inside your organization – like you – they count on you to help get the answers they need. If this requires that you refer your customer to another person or department, that's OK. Just do it in a way that lets your customer know that he or she *did* reach the right person the first time. And that person is...you.

Action Steps

Read these pages of the book out loud with other members of your department. Review your current procedures for answering calls, recording information and referring customer situations to one another. Apply the principles above to make your systems even better and your customers even more fulfilled.

Take the extra step, enjoy the extra business

Heather and Mark work at a leading attorneys' office in Seattle. They order fresh ground coffee for the office every month, and sent me this comparison between two major coffee vendors.

Coffee company 'Torrefazione' (I name the winners)

- We received a call from a customer service representative about a coffee order placed at their website earlier in the week.

- We were informed that shipments are sent by UPS, but their coffee warehouse is only a few blocks from our office. So they offered to send future orders via courier the next day without a shipping charge.

- They also noted we order coffee monthly and provided information on how we could qualify for a frequent customer discount.

Coffee company '********' (the losers know who they are)

- We had problems ordering ground coffee from their website.

- By default we ordered over the phone during office hours.

- One telephone representative asked us, 'Why don't you just go to one of our retail stores to buy the coffee?'

Guess which coffee company this attorneys' office now patronizes each and every month?

＊　＊　＊

Abdul Rahman is one of my students based in Singapore. He was visiting a nearby country when his wife's purse was stolen, including her credit cards from two different Singapore banks. Before he could report them stolen, they were used by someone else. He reports two totally different service experiences:

UOB Bank (I name the winners)

- $650 fraudulent charges

- The bank expressed sympathy at our predicament and assured us they would do their best in investigating the case.

- They asked if we could scan and e-mail the police report instead of sending by regular mail so that they could investigate immediately. (I did.)

- They called back immediately after receiving the e-mail and promised to get back to us as soon as possible.

- A few weeks later, the bank called and explained that their investigation showed the signature on the charge slips was different from the cardholder's. Therefore, all charges had been reversed.

*** Bank (the losers know who they are)

- $65 fraudulent charges

- I was told by someone at the bank, 'Our minimum charge for lost cards is $100 so you'd better pay the $65. Otherwise, we'll charge you $100.' (He must think I am an idiot.)

- After a loud outburst from me, he admitted that I am only liable for $65.

- I asked whether the bank, out of goodwill, can absorb this amount. He told us to write in and make the request.

- When asked whether we should send the letter to him, he replied that he was 'not yet in charge' of this case and that we should just mail the letter to '*** Bank Cards'.

- One week later I followed up. They said, 'No, we have not received any letter from you.'

- I faxed the original letter together with a cover letter explaining that the original was sent to them earlier.

- I called them to confirm if the fax was received.

- A few weeks later the same person called us from the bank at 8:30 am and said, 'We think you'd better pay the $65.'

- I mentioned the other bank's investigation showed the charges were fraudulent. He replied, 'Different banks have different policies.'

- When asked if we could appeal, he replied, 'You have appealed twice so it's not likely to be accepted.' (Our lost original letter and subsequent faxed copy of the same letter equals two appeals?)

- One week later, a letter from the bank arrived stating, 'Our investigation shows that you lost your card on April 13, but the report was only made on April 14. As such, you are liable for the minimum payment of $65.' From the tone of the letter, we speculate that nothing was actually done to investigate.

- I called the Fraud Control Department but was not allowed to speak to the person responsible for our case. I was told, 'He's busy.'

- Finally, we conceded and made the $65 payment.

Guess which bank Abdul patronizes today, and will continue to patronize enthusiastically tomorrow? Guess which bank his family will avoid?

Key Learning Point

Coffee company '********' and Singapore bank '***' are both very big in their markets. They are major players with many customers, huge budgets and profits (for now). But big bureaucracies can quickly become impersonal and remote. Staff can become more interested in doing things easily for themselves and pleasing their bosses, than serving their customers with a smile.

Meanwhile, smaller players who want more market share, greater customer loyalty and positive word of mouth can teach their staff to be pleasant, helpful, motivated and appreciative toward those who really count – the customers.

Action Steps

Ask yourself which are you right now: Are you the big dog who risks losing touch with your market? Or the underdog, keen to run an extra mile and keep your customers delighted?

Big dogs don't have to lose touch, but they have to work harder to keep their staff focused on genuine customer care. There's always room for an underdog – or a big dog – to be a bit more sensitive, more innovative and more helpful. Customers will notice and tell others all about it.

Why quality assurance is not enough

How can a company produce zero-defect products, boast dramatic cycle-time reductions, be certified for consistent, reliable performance...and still lose valuable customers?

Doesn't the systematic effort to reduce waste, improve yields and streamline processes lead to better service, higher profits and more loyal customers?

The answer is 'not necessarily'. Here's why:

Quality Assurance (QA) efforts such as ISO Certification, Six Sigma Quality Control and 10X Cycle-Time Reduction can lead to greater consistency, lower costs and higher speed. But these programs alone will not keep your finger on the ever-changing pulse of your customers' interests, hopes, needs, fears and feelings.

QA leads to greater predictability and higher standards. That's important!

But customers are human. And humans are intrigued by creativity, appreciation, personal touch, extra-mile efforts and surprise. That's important, too.

To win with customers in today's competitive world, you need both.

You've got to work on both continuously. You've got to be on time, and turned on. You've got to be accurate, and passionate. You've got to meet standards, and exceed expectations. You've got to please your customer, and sometimes tease your customer.

Key Learning Point

You must always improve your systems, methods, standards and procedures. But you must also cultivate the human qualities of intimacy, connection, caring, personality and style. Yes, squeeze those defects out the door, but keep the window open! Let your humanity come shining in.

Action Steps

Review the active improvement efforts at your organization. You should have ongoing QA programs featuring hard statistics, real experiments and rigorous workflow mapping. At the same time, you must have 'soft skills' programs to improve listening, personal communication, cultural respect, ethics, responsibility, recovery, service mindset and customer delight. Make sure you have a healthy mix of both for the success of your business, your employees and your customers.

Test yourself: How can you add more value?

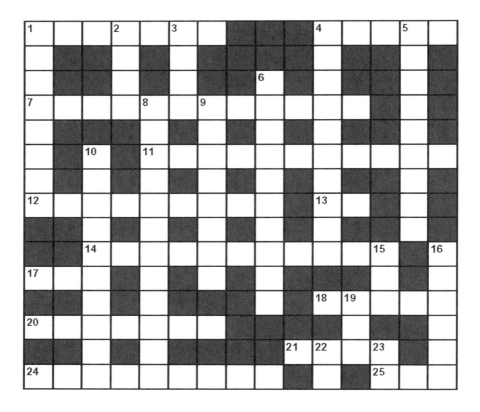

Answers in the Appendix. How many can you get before you look?

Puzzle clues

Across

1   Strong feeling or emotion
4   Treat badly
7   Payment for a service or loss
11   Setting in order, in advance
12   Able to accomplish a task
13   Information technology (abbr.)
14   Time-honored; orthodox
17   Happiness
18   Enter data
20   Move a person to a higher position; champion
21   Not functioning; gloomy
24   To enlarge beyond the truth
25   Belonging to us

Down

1   ____ makes perfect
2   Action as progress toward a goal
3   Receptive to new ideas
4   ____ increases productivity
5   Do this for a rainy day (two words)
6   Discuss and prepare a plan
8   Dickens's 'Great ____'
9   Explicit; in detail
10   Area without risk (two words)
15   Pay ____ service to
16   Published writer
19   Without delay or hesitation
22   Operational
23   Negative response

CHAPTER

3

LITTLE THINGS MEAN A LOT

If you think the little things don't matter, you haven't
been bitten by a mosquito or stung by a bee!

You are vulnerable at your lowest perception point

If you do your job well, your company will prosper and customers will return, right?

Not necessarily. It depends on how well your colleagues and teammates do their jobs, too.

You may be the best chef in town with fresh ingredients and fabulous food, but if the waiters in your restaurant are surly and rude, your customers won't come back.

Your chef may be great and the waiters impeccably polite, but if your cleaner leaves the restrooms a mess, your customers won't come back.

Your chef may be world-class, your waiters polite and the restrooms sparkling clean. But if your service is s-l-o-w or the billing is wrong, your customers won't come back.

Your entire enterprise is vulnerable at the lowest 'perception point' your customers experience or discover: your slowest system, dirtiest floor, darkest corner, worst driver, least-competent technician or most unfriendly staff.

This is true for organizations. It's also true for individuals.

Have you ever been served by someone capable and skilled, but with strong body odor or bad breath? Would you gladly call on them again for service? Have you ever been served by someone friendly, patient and caring, but technically incompetent or clueless? Would you trust them to serve you again?

Whatever is your worst, lowest or least, that is where your service reputation will thrive, dive or barely survive. Find the lowest point in your organization, your department or your life – and bring it up.

Key Learning Point

Customers form their opinions through a series of 'perception points'; every moment as they see, hear, touch, feel, smell or taste your products, people, packaging, places, promotions, policies and procedures. Your entire business is vulnerable at the lowest point in that chain.

Action Steps

Review every point of customer contact. Start with your products and systems. Identify everything that is obsolete, incorrect, difficult to read, hard to use, confusing or just plain ugly. Choose the worst and make it better.

Next, examine your people. Find those who are slow, late, uncaring, unpleasant, unmotivated, impatient or just plain rude. Teach them, train them, coach them, motivate them, reward them, encourage them, inspire them. But if all that doesn't work, then just let them go.

Finally, examine yourself. Where are you late, sloppy, inefficient, ineffective or incomplete? Pick one area you can improve this month and take the action you need to improve it.

The words you choose to use

I choose words every day. When speaking, writing, requesting and deciding, I use some words and not others. You do, too.

The words we choose create meaning and mission in our lives. This became clear when a close friend said he was 'still looking for a wife'. I know this guy. He will only get married when he decides to stop looking – and start finding.

Listen to the difference in these few words:

'What do you want?' or 'How may I help you?'

'I didn't mean it.' or 'Please accept my apology.'

'It's in the instruction manual.' or 'Let me answer that for you.'

'We don't have any more.' or 'I can order that for you now.'

What a difference a few words can make!

*   *   *

In the bathroom of Le Meridien Cyberport Hotel in Hong Kong, I found a small note with a stern message. In bold letters it said:

> I FORGOT: Should you need other amenities, please do not hesitate to call our Solutions Center. Press '0'.
>
> - Sewing Kit - Nail Kit - Razor Kit
>
> - Dental Kit - Shoe Mitt - Mouth Wash
>
> - Hair Kit - Others

I checked my toiletries and was relieved that I did not forget. It doesn't sound very inviting to call a 'Solutions Center' and request a 'dental kit'.

One week later in the bathroom of the Crowne Plaza Hotel in Dubai, I found a small note with a gentle message:

WITH OUR COMPLIMENTS: If you require any essential toiletries, please contact reception. We will be pleased to deliver to you with our compliments: shaving cream, razor, comb, toothbrush and toothpaste, cotton wool or female sanitary products. Welcome home.

As I read the note, I felt comfortable, cared for and at ease.

What a difference a few words can make!

*   *   *

On a boat in Hawaii, the crew was unfriendly and rude. A large sign read: 'Wind and waves can tip the boat, but only you can tip the crew.' There were sixteen tourists on board. Not one left a tip.

At a coffee bar in Malaysia, I saw a box with a sign reading 'Tips are encouraged', but I saw no smiles from the staff. The tip box was empty.

On Starbucks counters worldwide, small boxes are full of coins and notes – tips for the enthusiastic team. No sign is needed: Genuine smiles and friendly service send the appropriate message.

In the rooms at the Sofitel in Hanoi there is a sign: 'During your stay we would be grateful if you respect our "no tipping" policy. Your satisfaction is our best reward.'

What a difference a smile can make.

*   *   *

You can also teach key words and special phrases to your customers. This will increase their sense of belonging, loyalty and connection.

It took months of practice, but I can now walk confidently into Starbucks and ask for 'a tall, low-fat, double-shot mocha with a single pump and extra whip, not too hot'. (Which means a medium-sized drink with an extra shot of espresso, one third the usual amount of chocolate syrup, low-fat milk steamed to a slightly lower temperature than usual, plenty of whipped cream on top.)

* * *

Choose special words and phrases to communicate with colleagues and not offend your clients.

At Disney stores worldwide, good buyers are called 'Guests' and potential trouble makers or shoplifters are called 'Customers'. It's very helpful when staff need to point out someone to the store manager or security guard. They simply say out loud, 'A customer here needs help!' raising their first finger upwards with their thumb pointing in the direction of the potentially problematic 'customer'.

* * *

When will software designers realize that 'Search' is a database function, while 'Find' is what people want to accomplish?

Every word has mood and meaning. Every word counts.

* * *

Choose your words carefully when asking staff for feedback after a training session.

The evaluation form I use features just three questions, each focusing on the value, benefit and application of the new learning:

a. What did you learn today that you found most beneficial?

b. How will you apply what you have learned at work?

c. Any other comments are welcome.

I do not recommend any question that causes participants to judge the training (e.g., Not Satisfied, Somewhat Satisfied, Very Satisfied). This turns your students into critics at the last minute when they should be focusing most clearly on reviewing key points and planning their action steps.

If your participants do have praise, suggestions or complaints about the training or the speaker/trainer, they will use the 'comments' section provided.

Key Learning Point

Every word and phrase you choose conveys mood, tone and meaning. Remember, customers and colleagues come in every possible stage of enthusiasm, anxiety, understanding and confusion. Pay attention! When you are offering, asking, responding, explaining, invoicing, installing or advising, choose the words you use with care.

Action Steps

From your customers' point of view, which words and phrases sound positive and helpful, appreciative and respectful, inviting and secure? Which words sound cold and confusing, overly technical or even condescending? Make a list.

Now review the language of your company communications. Read everything aloud. Listen to the words as they are spoken. Do you hear what customers love to hear, or do you hear internal conversations, industry standards and company jargon? Listen carefully to your language and then improve it.

It takes one grump to spoil a brand!

Companies invest millions to create, design, fine-tune, build, promote and extend their brands. Think Nike, Virgin, Versace, Raffles, Amazon.

All your investment brings customers to your door (or website) with expectations matching your promotional promise. But when customer meets company 'face-to-face', everything hinges on that critical moment.

A friend recently moved to Singapore from Australia and went shopping for an appropriate wardrobe. I saw her several hours into the spending spree and heard her say, 'I love Liz Claiborne, but E—T (a competing brand) can take their clothes and shove it.' (Australians can be oh-so-delicate in their speech.) She continued, 'I won't *ever* go in one of *their* stores again.'

Wow! That's strong stuff. Turns out a sales lady at 'E' couldn't be bothered to say hello or help my friend with her questions. She was too busy with a personal call on her mobile phone. And when she hung up, she chatted about the call with her colleague (distracting the colleague from yet another customer) rather than responding to the queries of my friend.

To this day, the 'E' brand of clothing is like an enemy in the mall, a regular reminder to my friend of the 'who cares?' attitude, poor manners and disrespect.

I wonder what the designers, marketing team, logistics office, production operators, backroom and warehouse staff would think of that person on the front lines who couldn't be bothered to give good service? If they could meet her face-to-face, what would they say about her performance? If you were that lady's boss, what would you say?

Terrence Nielsen, store manager of IKEA in Singapore, knows exactly what he'd say. He tells his staff every day, 'If you don't feel like coming to work...don't! The last thing we need is to have anyone at work bringing down the mood for our customers and everyone else. If you don't feel good about yourself and your job, stay home!'

Key Learning Point

One grump can spoil a brand. Don't let that grumpy person be you! The reputation of your entire company, the livelihood of all your colleagues and the success of your business and your brand depend on you.

Action Steps

Check your mood and attitude every day when you go to work. Check it again during the morning, after lunch and in the afternoon. If you are not looking, feeling and sounding 100% like someone *you* would like to meet, go back to the restroom, go back to lunch, go back to sleep. Don't go to work and spoil everyone else's day.

Should you crack the tough nuts?

Years ago I used to focus on the worst members of the audience. The ones who crossed their arms and legs, never smiled, hardly said a word or took a single note throughout the day. I felt the need to 'win them over' to prove my ability as a speaker and a trainer.

I've learned something over the years: Some people do not want to be won over – and that's OK.

Now I focus on the audience members who *do* respond with smiling, nodding, taking notes, asking questions and laughing along with my stories. This gives me a lot more energy when I work, and also makes those participants feel appreciated.

And guess what? By the end of my presentations, most of the tough nuts have cracked themselves. Even tough nuts sometimes want to join the party – but they don't want someone else to do the cracking.

This can be equally true with members of your staff or service team. Some people inside your organization can be real tough nuts, sticks-in-the-mud, fuddy duddies, old-timers, or even new-timers who don't want to support a change, improvement or new program.

What should you do? Should you work extra hard to win them over? I suggest otherwise.

Instead of focusing on the few who don't want to support new ideas, focus on those who are enthusiastic, helpful, optimistic about change and generally inclined to make new things work.

Think about it: Every ounce of energy you put into the enthusiastic members of your team comes back to you in support, ideas, action, initiative and positive effort. Every ounce of energy you put into the 'tough nuts' gets you what? A worn-out nutcracker.

Here's one example: A prestigious hospital asked me to help improve the morale among the nurses in the operating theaters. There were 86 nurses on the team, but senior managers were most concerned with four long-serving staff who had become negative and reluctant.

I studied the situation carefully and recommended they ignore those unwilling or uninterested in change. Instead, we focused every ounce of effort on working with those nurses who wanted to work toward a better culture.

Within months, three of the tough nuts loosened up and started contributing good ideas. They were welcomed with appreciation for their wisdom and the quality of their contributions.

The other tough nut never cracked; she left the hospital and went to work elsewhere. Funny thing, within a few months, no one missed her.

Key Learning Point

In life, with staff, customers and everyone else on this planet, some will be keen and helpful and eager to see you win – and others will not. Be careful where you focus.

Action Steps

Identify which of your staff are most constructive and helpful in bringing new plans to light. Tell them how much you appreciate their efforts and support. You will find you get even more. Don't ignore the tough nuts, just don't give them any more attention than they require. In time they will join the successful crowd, or they will leave. In which case, let them go.

Business busters and loyalty losers

My friend flew business class with her two-year-old son on a four and a half hour journey. Three hours into the flight the boy became fidgety and loud. My friend asked the stewardess if there was a coloring book or other child's toy onboard.

The stewardess went to check and returned with this response: 'Yes, we do have giveaway kits on board for small children.'

'May I have one please?' my friend asked.

'I'm sorry,' was the reply, 'the children's giveaway kits are only for flights above five hours.'

New title for this stewardess? Customer Alienator.

*   *   *

When my daughter Brighten was eight years old we were shopping together in an attractive clothing store. The shirts and pants on display were the right size and absolutely the right color for her.

A young saleswoman approached, looked at my daughter and asked immediately, 'How old is she?'

I was shocked by her aggressive tone and replied defensively, 'Why do you want to know?'

She repeated her question. 'How old is she?'

'What difference does it make?' I asked, now perturbed.

'We only have clothing for up to six years old,' she replied with a snap.

Since when does the age of a customer make more sense than the fit of the clothing?

New title for this saleswoman? Business Buster.

*   *   *

A well-known fast-food restaurant offers 'Teen Discount Cards' to attract more young customers from 2:30 to 6:00 pm (a slow period between lunch and dinner).

One day a young customer joined a long and slow-moving line at 5:50 pm, patiently waiting his turn. But when he got to the counter it was 6:05 pm. The supervisor said his discount card was no longer valid.

The young man (and his friend) walked out and into the restaurant next door.

New title for this supervisor? Value Vaporizer.

*   *   *

Vineet from India wrote about a coffee shop that gave away free *hot* drinks when customers filled their 'frequent customer cards', but wouldn't give away *iced* coffee drinks. This continued until a new staff member pointed out to the manager that adding ice doesn't raise costs – but does raise customer delight.

Someone should put a few ice cubes down that manager's pants! And when he is wide awake, teach him this key point: Cutting costs should be the last thing on your mind when rewarding your loyal customers, the ones you want returning again and again. Generosity going out equals profits coming in.

New title for this manager? Loyalty Loser.

*   *   *

Clancey in Dubai took his son Denis to an ice cream parlor for dessert. When his son stepped into the parking lot the ice cream fell out of his cone – plop! – onto the ground. The boy began to cry.

Clancey walked back into the store and told the clerk what happened. The clerk took a new cone, packed in a new scoop of ice cream, then turned it upside down and handed it to Clancey. With a stern look and a sterner voice he said, 'Our ice cream doesn't fall out of the cone.'

Someone should put a scoop of ice cream down that clerk's pants! And when he's wide awake, teach him this key point: Never make your customer feel wrong, stupid or untrusted.

New title for this clerk? Enjoyment Eliminator.

Instead, with a smile on your face say joyfully, 'Here's a brand-new cone for you. I packed it in extra tight this time – just to make sure you and your son will enjoy every lick. And thank you for coming back in. See you again soon!'

✳   ✳   ✳

My friend sent his inkjet printer to the manufacturer for repair. The service center technician sent him an e-mail with estimated charges and asked him to print it out, sign it and fax it back to approve charges for the service prior to making the repair.

How could my friend print out the e-mail when the service center already had his printer?

New title for this technician: Absurdity Agent.

✳   ✳   ✳

My neighbor prefers white hens eggs as opposed to brown ones, but they were hard to find in our local grocery store. After not seeing them at all for several weeks, she asked the manager why.

He replied, 'The white eggs were selling out so fast that we had trouble keeping them in stock. So we quit carrying them.'

New title for this manager: Marketing Mistake.

✳   ✳   ✳

Two close friends enjoyed an extraordinary world-class cruise. The cruise company worked hard to personalize the vacation for everyone on board. Pre-cruise telephone calls identified each traveler's likes and dislikes, hopes, dreams and concerns regarding the upcoming voyage.

Onboard the ship, the staff memorized every passenger's name. Personal preferences were rigorously recorded and used to upgrade the intimacy of service every day.

On the final morning, a questionnaire was slipped under the door of my friends' cabin asking for feedback and suggestions for improvement. The first three questions on the form were:

Your name:

Your cabin:

Today's date:

An entire cruise devoted to impeccable, personal service, and one impersonal, generic form at the end reminds guests that they are not really so special after all.

New title for the survey specialist: Anonymity Enhancer.

* * *

I visited a coffee shop where the staff was apologetic but unwilling to give me one free coffee drink even though my 'Frequent Customer Card' was all filled up. (Their 'special promotion' expired one day before, while it took me two weeks to fill the card from a series of ten paid drinks.)

The frontline staff said they would love to give me the drink, but 'management' told them not to.

I was so perturbed by the lack of generosity and frontline empowerment that I avoided that brand for months.

Notes to coffee bean counters:

1. Cost of giving away one free drink = pennies in ground beans, paper cup and hot water.

2. Value of lost business from one unhappy coffee drinker = many dollars.

I shared this experience with many friends (upset customers usually do). One told me how pleased he was when 'someone with a brain' gave him a free drink even though the promotion had expired. Another said he got a free drink and was given a cookie, too! Both promised to patronize their outlets for months to come.

Notes to coffee bean counters:

1. Cost of giving away one free cookie = less than a dollar.

2. Value of repeat business from happy coffee drinkers = endless.

3. Value of positive word-of-mouth = you can't ever buy such credible and powerful promotion.

If the purpose of a promotion is to encourage repeat business, why even have an expiration date? Who cares *when* customers buy their drinks, as long as they keep buying and drinking and drinking and buying?

New name for these out-of-date coffee bean counters: Profit Reduction Specialists.

Key Learning Point

Every business has procedures, policies, products, packaging, pricing, places and promotions. But *people* hold the ultimate key to customer experience, loyalty and delight.

One smart cookie beats a bureaucratic full house. Give your customers positive pleasure, not pesky problems. They will return and reward you.

Action Steps

The next time your customer confronts the stupidity of a policy that doesn't make sense, or the absurdity of a procedure that just doesn't work, be the person who can and does make a difference.

Speak up! Stand out! Champion your customer's cause. Take a stand for common sense in your business. Be the one to stir the pot. Remember, your company's pot (not the policy manual) fills your bowl every morning.

When service goes wrong, bounce back!

We all try to do things right. No business sets out to do wrong when servicing customers. But life is full of unexpected moments and, inevitably, mistakes do happen.

While many people in business focus on doing things right the first time, very few seem to take a powerful interest in setting things right when things do go wrong. In those moments, a passion for 'zero defects' often gives way to 'Let's get this mess cleaned up fast and pretend it never happened.'

Because of this attitude, businesses miss an important opportunity to build customer loyalty and valuable goodwill. It is exactly when things go *wrong* that customers are most sensitive about how they are treated, most likely to share their experiences with friends and colleagues and most likely to make lasting decisions about whether to bring their future business back to that company, or to its rival.

We all know mistakes will happen. What we do not know is how we will be treated when we go back to get the mistake corrected. 'Will they treat me as if it's my fault?' 'Will they argue with me?' 'Will they make it difficult for me to prove my purchase, fill out papers or otherwise file my complaint?'

In these unpleasant moments, customers' sensitivities are

heightened. If they were casual shoppers before, they become discerning now. If they were discerning shoppers before, they become hypersensitive when things go awry.

You can make that sensitivity work in your favor. When service errors are quickly and professionally handled, customer loyalty can actually 'bounce back' to greater heights than if the problem never happened. That's why service recovery situations can be described as 'opportunities you wish you never had'.

Consider this example:

You buy a pair of expensive shoes at a small boutique and pay cash. You go home and eventually throw away the receipt. Two weeks later as you're walking down the street, the heel pops off and falls beyond reach into the drain below. You decide to return your new shoes to the boutique and ask for a replacement. But of course you're a bit nervous since you've thrown away your receipt.

Now imagine the sales clerk welcoming you with a smile and right away setting you at ease about not having kept your receipt. She promptly gives you a new pair of shoes and then adds in a free pair of matching socks to thank you for coming back, and to apologize for the inconvenience you experienced.

Would you return to that boutique in the future? Would you recommend that boutique to your friends? Of course you would. Your loyalty to the boutique has actually gone *up* because you had a service problem and the recovery was handled very well.

This is the key point: When things go wrong, you have a tremendous opportunity to build *more* customer loyalty just by quickly and generously setting things right.

To capture the secret advantage hiding inside your next service breakdown, train everyone to understand and use these seven simple steps to gain customer loyalty.

'Bouncing Back' with S E R V I C E recovery:

S-ay You're Sorry.

There's nothing like a sincere apology, delivered right away, to let people know you really care. There's no need to grovel or apologize forever. One honest and heartfelt apology will suffice.

E-xpedite Solutions.

The faster you can fix the problem, the better. This is not the time to calculate the cost of repairing the damage. Do what it takes to set things right. Costs will be forgotten or absorbed over time, but benefits last forever.

R-espond to the Customer.

Remember people are involved, not just products, dates and orders. Take the time to empathize. Be a listening ear. Keep personal contact; use the phone, send a fax, stay in touch. And when it's all over, thank them personally with a note, small gift or some other special gesture.

V-ictory to the Customer.

Build higher levels of customer loyalty by giving more than they expect. Refunds, discounts, special assistance, extra services; it doesn't have to be money. But whatever it is, do it fast! No loyalty is gained from a refund or gesture that takes months to negotiate, authorize or discuss.

I-mplement Improvements.

Change your processes and improve training to avoid the same problem next time. Institutionalize improvements.

C-ommunicate Results.

Spread the word so that everyone can learn from what has happened. Provide full information about consequences and improvements.

E-xtend the Outcome.

Don't stop working when they stop complaining. Stay in touch until you are sure the customer comes back and their long-term loyalty is assured.

What else can you do to keep your customers coming back for more?

Make it easy for your customers to complain! Create new ways for customers to let you know what's wrong.

Here are some ideas to get you started:

- Set up a telephone hotline for immediate response to customer comments and complaints.

- Give counter staff the power to take prompt and significant action for your customers.

- Conduct focus groups with a cross-section of customers to find out what they want you to improve.

- Run surveys to keep track of your customers' changing expectations. Find out what customers are buying now and what they want in the future.

- Provide easy-to-use comment cards at all points of customer contact and insert them in all outgoing mail. Show your appreciation for responses, and reply quickly.

- Become a customer of your best competitors. Eagerly seek out what they do better or differently than you. Then make appropriate improvements in your business operation.

Long-term, loyal customers lead to lower costs, repeat orders, frequent referrals and expanding profit margins. Losing one of these precious patrons is much more costly than the revenue from a single sale!

Service recovery does cost money (although a sincere apology costs nothing and goes a long way toward appeasing upset customers). But perhaps service recovery shouldn't be seen as a cost at all!

Bouncing back through generous service recovery is a proven strategy for building repeat business and long-term sustainable profits. It's not a cost, it's an intelligent business investment.

Take the quiz: What are the little things that mean a lot?

Answers in the Appendix...but ask a friend for help before you peek!

Puzzle clues

<u>Across</u>

1	Prevent; bar
2	Carry out or perform
3	An affirmative
7	Deep perceptions
9	State explicitly; fine point
10	Most agreeable or pleasing
11	Carry out
12	Not scheduled for duties
13	Approval
15	Set of rules
16	Way of thinking and behaving
18	Get or derive
20	Approve
21	Helpful

<u>Down</u>

1	____ like a bee
2	Failed to meet expectations
4	Disgrace
5	Reponses to problems
6	Business that serves other businesses
8	Providers; intermediaries
9	Range and variety
10	____ a doubt
12	Introducing an alternative
14	Forward motion
15	Concern for others
16	Evoke a response
17	Develop through experience
19	What one swears
22	Raise your service level

CHAPTER

4

GOING THE EXTRA MILE

What makes one person stand out from the others? The willingness to go the distance – and then keep on going!

How to avoid competing on price

I helped a company that sells computer disks and hard drives directly to consumers.

The global market is flooded with these commodity products, and with companies eager to sell them.

They asked me, 'How can we avoid lowering our price when other suppliers are always ready to drop their price lower than ours? How can we cultivate customer loyalty without discounting ourselves right out of business?'

The answer to this dilemma was to deliver more *value* than companies who compete only on price. But how do you add more value when the product is a commodity?

This company became a fountain of useful ideas, timely information, practical suggestions, cost-effective checklists, interesting case studies and best-practice techniques.

This hard drive company sends customers and prospects monthly e-mail messages of *value*, including:

- Reminders to back up critical data weekly (who sends that message to you?)

- Proven ideas on how to manage volumes of data easily in folders, files and storage libraries

- Rotation patterns for data backups with the benefits and drawbacks of each approach

- Easy ways to gain user participation in safe computing and data backup procedures

- A comparison of various options for backing up data onto disks, tape drives, CDs or websites

- Current case studies of major computer crashes and restoration results

- Ideas for backing up and synchronizing your data while at home or on the road

- Screen savers reminding users to back up their data regularly

- Cost analyses of doing data recovery and restoration with and without current backups

- Techniques for keeping paper backups to correspond with digital records

- Interesting milestones in the history of hard drives and information on the latest in data storage technology

Of course they don't give ALL this information to every customer or prospect all at once. Rather, they trickle it out over time, keeping their company top-of-mind throughout the year and first-in-mind when their prospects and customers are ready to buy.

Key Learning Point

Focusing on product and price keeps you in the same arena as every other vendor, scratching each other with deep discounts until everyone bleeds red ink. Don't go there! Instead, build a better reputation by informing, educating, managing and motivating your customers to think frequently *about* you and then to take their buying actions *to* you.

Action Steps

Think of the ways customers use and abuse your products and services. What are the top tips for getting maximum value? What are the most common mistakes? Put these insights into easy-to-follow checklists. Write a 'best-practice case study' revealing how your smartest customers create maximum business value. Has your company grown, changed or improved over time? Explain this in a story that highlights your continuous commitment. Take these articles and send them out by e-mail, post them on your website, insert them with your products. Don't reduce your everyday prices – increase your everyday value!

A well-informed customer is a *better* customer

When customers know what to do, how to do it, what to expect and why, they usually follow instructions.

When customers are uncertain about what, how or why, they will often hesitate in uncertainty and doubt.

This can be a major problem, especially when customer participation is essential to your success.

For example, medicines not taken on time will degrade the quality of a patient's recovery and healing. Automobiles with oil not changed will wear down before their time. Lawns not watered by owners after fresh fertilization will burn in the sun and die. Data backups not performed on time result in very angry customers when their hard drives unfortunately but inevitably crash.

Since customer performance and participation is so important (it's called compliance in medical terms), you'd think everyone would put more effort into educating customers about exactly what to do and motivating them to do it. Remarkably, this is often not the case.

Buy an inexpensive alarm clock and you'll get a 12-page user's manual on how to set the time, change the battery and work every feature of the alarm. But buy $96 worth of prescription drugs and you might get a little sticker on the bottle saying something cryptic like '1C 3X w/meals'.

A pharmacist will explain that '1C 3X w/meals' means 'Take 1 capsule, 3 times a day, with your meals.' A doctor may also advise if the medicine is best taken before or after your meals. (The cryptic code gives no clue.) They may even warn you of possible side effects and what you can do about them. (None of this useful information is found on the little sticker.)

How many people receive medication every day, but they are nervous or unwell when their doctor or pharmacist explains it to them? Back home they may forget what was said, and then they are left with only the little sticker reading '1C 3X w/meals'.

Under these circumstances, some patients will forget what to do, when to do it and why. They may feel uncertain and hesitate. In medical terms, they may not fully comply.

Consider the consequences for the doctor (an unwell patient), for the pharmacy (a dissatisfied customer), for the hospital (a complaint to be answered) and for the patient (a continued illness, discomfort or frustration). In short, a very bad situation.

How easily this could be avoided by making a better effort to inform, educate and motivate the customer! (Every company can find a way to do this better, including yours.)

For example:

The drug manufacturer could provide an easy-to-understand flyer or brochure with every medication. The doctor could create a simple list of what to take, what to expect and what to avoid. The pharmacy could design an attractive calendar to hang on the bathroom mirror or refrigerator door. The calendar could include space for you to 'check the boxes' and track your daily participation. The hospital could maintain a website with up-to-date information and helpful FAQs – and print the website address right on the bottle's little sticker.

A smart computer company could send out an e-mail once a day with a simple reminder: *'Back up your data now!'* They could send another reminder at the end of the week with a checklist of costs in time and expense to recreate your data from scratch.

A lawn care company could provide a simple notepad with every page reminding you of the next time and date to water your fertilized lawn. They could add two photographs to keep you motivated: one lush, green and beautiful; the other dry, parched and pathetic.

A car maintenance company could put a bright sticker on the cap of your gas tank asking: 'Is it time to change your oil?' They might even include a note like this: 'Bring your auto in on time and save 10%.'

The bank could send you an e-mail one week before your term deposit matures or when your checking account approaches the minimum required balance. A link in the message could take you to the right web page where you can extend your deposit, increase your balance or transfer funds as required.

Key Learning Point

Customer participation is a key to achieving high levels of loyalty and satisfaction. Earn this participation by giving your customers the information, education and motivation they need. Do it at the right time, in the right amount, at the right place and in the most engagingly effective manner. (Hint to pharmacists and doctors: a little sticker on the bottle isn't it.)

Action Steps

Improve the quantity, quality, consistency, frequency, accuracy and attractiveness of the information you provide to your customers this month.

Work on improving your handouts, flyers, e-mails, checklists, informative posters and brochures, stickers and decals, manuals, user guides, videos, web pages, guidelines and instructions.

Do a better job of telling customers what to do, bring, prepare, submit, copy, file, track, complete and expect. Tell them more about the time, steps, costs, input, output, problems, indicators and guarantors of success. Make them better informed, better educated and better motivated. In short, make them better customers.

How to make your service better

Kim in Colorado posed this question: 'How do you find time to work on customer service when each day is already filled with seemingly impossible to complete tasks?'

The answer lies in the difference between working *in* customer service and working *on* customer service.

Working *in* customer service means taking care of your customers – always a good idea. Customers appreciate the attention and you feel good providing quality service. Being *in* service takes a specific amount of your time to benefit a specific customer in a specific way.

Working *on* your customer service is totally different. It means creating, changing, improving or fine-tuning the tools, systems and procedures you use when you are working *in* service for others.

Here's a personal example:

Several years ago a magazine editor in Europe interviewed me by telephone for an article on 'Building an Uplifting Service Culture'. He asked me to send him a high-quality color photograph to run with the article. I went right to work *in* service. I chose an existing photograph from my files, had a high-quality color copy made overnight, contacted a courier company and had the photograph on his desk two days later. The whole process took a few hours of my time and made the editor very happy.

The following week I went to work *on* my customer service. I chose 22 photographs, had them all scanned as high-resolution images and posted them on my website so that anyone, anywhere, anytime can choose the photo they want, in high or low resolution, and have it downloaded directly to their computer or sent instantly to their e-mail address as an attachment.

The whole process took a few hours of my time and has since made many editors and meeting planners very happy. Want to see it work? Click to:

http://www.RonKaufman.com/media/images/index.html

It's easy to get very busy *in* customer service. Without even trying, your day is filled with seemingly impossible-to-complete tasks. Working *on* your customer service is different. It also takes your time, but it continues to serve after you have moved on to something or someone else.

Key Learning Point

Everyone who works *in* service for others should also work *on* their customer service. If you improve your service system just a little each week, those small improvements can make a big difference over time. And if you work *on* your service in a cross-functional team or over a weekend retreat, imagine how much everyone (customers and service providers) will gain.

Action Steps

Step back from working *in* service and go to work *on* your service. Make a checklist, design a form, create a template. Reduce four steps to three, or even one. Invest some time each week working *on* your service, then go back to work *in* service. You may still be very busy – but everything will be running a bit smoother, a bit easier, a bit better.

Tweak your customer or tweak your system?

The Disneyland Hotel recently tarnished Mickey's reputation with an influential customer from Seattle. Mark stayed at a hotel inside the park with his family for three days. He attended a legal seminar while his family enjoyed Disney rides, ate Disney meals and spent at Disney plenty! His seminar ended at noon on the third day, but hotel checkout was 11:00 am.

On the second night Mark asked for a late check-out until 1:00 or 2:00 pm the following day. Staff at the front desk refused to give him an answer. They said it was too late and he would have to ask again at 7:00 am.

Mark was in the lobby promptly at 7:00 am. But when he asked for a short check-out extension, the front office manager flatly refused. He said, 'If I give you a late check out, others will want one, too.'

Mark appealed for just two hours to complete his seminar and get his family with small children safely packed and out of the room. The manager replied, 'If you leave late, you'll mess up the schedule for our cleaners.'

Ouch! So much for customer service when leaving the House of the Mouse. Too bad the front office manager didn't know that last impressions are lasting impressions.

In contrast...

Raffles Hotel now has a policy of flexible check-in and check-out so their valued guests may enjoy a full 24-hour stay, no matter what time they check in, or out. Now that's convenient. That's hospitality. That's impeccable value and service.

'Raffles 24' is now available in all Raffles hotels and resorts. No wonder they are among the fastest-growing and most-admired brands in the world.

Note: Implementing this policy requires more communication between various teams and departments. But what are your staff and systems really for? Scheduling cleaners or taking care of customers?

Key Learning Point

The purpose of your staff and system is to serve your customers better. When customers make requests outside normal procedures, your job is to tweak the system, *not* the customer.

Action Steps

When customers ask for service outside your normal procedures, you have a choice: either teach your customers to follow procedures (through advance advice and information) or adapt your procedures to please your customers (through innovation and continuous improvement).

Is your survey worth my time?

A manufacturer complains that his customers rarely return the satisfaction surveys he sends out.

A leading resort gets back just 30% of the comment cards left for guests inside their fancy rooms.

One government agency had a response rate of only 6% when they sent out an 11-page survey.

What's going on here? Why is the response rate so low? Why don't customers complete and return customer satisfaction surveys?

The problem, as I see it, is twofold:

First, the format of many satisfaction surveys has taken on the language of academics and the structure of statisticians. Asking customers to rate the relative importance and performance, both perceived and expected, of 17 categories on a scale from 1 to 10 is a bit like asking someone attending the theater to evaluate the parking, lighting, sound system, seating, air conditioning, restrooms, refreshments and ushers – and, oh, by the way, did you enjoy the performance?

If your questionnaire is too complex for customers to understand at a glance, it's just too complex.

If your survey is too long for them to complete in a few quick minutes, it's just too long.

If your response form is loaded with jargon, scales and numbers, it's so filled up with *your* ideas there's no place left for your customers to speak their minds.

A statistical sampling of customer opinion can make sense. A quantitative monthly or quarterly survey may highlight where you're slipping, climbing or simply standing still.

But don't ask every customer to reply 'by the numbers', or the majority will *stop* thinking about your survey, before they even start!

That leads to the second point: Customers learned long ago that 'standard surveys' yield a 'standard company response' – which in many cases is nothing.

If I complete your survey, how can I be sure you'll take *action* on my comments? There's little guarantee of action in a long list of detailed questions, tiny little boxes and columns of numbers.

If you want to increase the quantity and value of customer comments you receive, if you want to make your survey really *work hard* for you, here are three things you can do:

First, make it clear at the top of your survey that your customer's comments are not just collected, they are truly valued.

'Customer Satisfaction Survey' is about as interesting as gray paint. *'Your Voice Counts!'* sounds much better. *'Tell us what you want!'* is appealing. *'We are listening to YOU!'* is a promise I'd reply to.

Second, design your form to gather qualitative input you will study and act on. Ask for subjective impressions and ideas with questions like these:

'What did you like? What didn't you like? What *would* you like? What do we do that you wish we didn't? What would you like us to change? What did you appreciate the most? What should we provide that is missing? Did anyone or anything let you down? How can we serve you even better? What do we have to do to justify raising our price by 10%? What does no one in our business do that you think everyone should do? What should we start doing, stop doing, do more of, do less of, do immediately?'

That's a long list to choose from. Pick the questions that work for you and use them! (A blank 'comments' field on your existing form just doesn't cut it!)

Third, promise – and then take – immediate action. Tell customers how *quickly* their comments will be read, and how *fast* the changes will occur.

Ask them: 'May we reply to you personally about this? If so, please check here.' Now it's obvious that you *are* reading every comment, you *are* listening to the customer, you *are* committed to making changes every day.

Key Learning Point

In today's busy world, your customer satisfaction survey must be so interesting and worthwhile that customers are glad to fill it in. If your survey is not engaging and attractive, customers will ignore it.

Action Steps

Look carefully at the design, format and length of your current customer satisfaction survey. Does it capture your customer's interest? Does it promise fast response and action? Should you change the name? the length? the questions? the design? Can you afford not to?

Your survey might be the last thing your customers see when doing business with you. Are you creating the right 'last impression'?

Are your frequent customers free-loaders, scoundrels or cheats?

Many companies reward their customers with a system for accumulating points with each purchase. These points are redeemable for free products or services in the future.

Fly enough on the same airline and you get a free ticket. Stay enough nights with the same hotel and you can enjoy free weekends. Rent cars from the same company again and again and free upgrades will be yours. Buy coffee or ice cream nine times in a row and the tenth cup or cone will be free.

This habit of gathering points is widespread and familiar, but customer experiences when redeeming these points are incredibly inconsistent. Some companies go out of their way to make you feel truly rewarded for the loyalty you have shown. Others treat you like a freeloader and dish out only the lowest level of service.

This is a cultural (and business) issue of the highest order. Here are a few examples:

An ice cream store ran a promotion to encourage frequent buyers. If you ate ice cream enough times during the promotional period, you earned a coupon for one free 'all-you-can-eat' session of indulgence the following month.

One of my students earned the coupon and went to enjoy his indulgence. The first scoop of ice cream was presented in an attractive glass bowl with a clean spoon. His second scoop was placed back into the same glass bowl, with a new spoon. The third scoop came back in the same glass bowl again, with the same old spoon. The fourth scoop was served in a paper cup with a small wooden spoon. The fifth scoop came back in the same paper cup with the same wooden spoon and a glower from the manager in charge.

My student did not stay for any further scoops in his 'all-you-can-eat' celebration...and has not returned to that store for ice cream again.

He noted, 'I felt humiliated by the staff, as though enjoying my all-you-can-eat prize was in some way cheating the store. Hadn't I earned my coupon? Didn't I deserve to enjoy the prize?'

One popular airline encourages frequent flying with 'double miles' promotions and special 'tier bonuses' for very frequent flyers. One of our subscribers tried to use her points to book a free award ticket in First Class, but the airline refused to confirm her reservation. The airline's approach was to *sell* the seats first to 'real' paying passengers, and then 'give the seats away' to frequent flyers if they were still available at the very last moment before departure.

How shortsighted! How does the airline think the passenger accumulated all those points in the first place? By flying as a 'real' paying passenger, of course!

Contrast this approach with the more enlightened view of Starwood Hotels and Resorts. Redeeming an award with Starwood is fast and easy, and the service you get in the hotel is especially warm and attentive. The Asia-Pacific Manager of Customer Care explained it to me this way: 'If someone has enjoyed an award before, they will strive to earn more points.'

Listen carefully to the language:

1. *Enjoyed an award* means Starwood makes a special effort to ensure the customer is pleased with his or her entire redemption experience: booking the award and enjoying the award.

2. *They will strive to earn more points* means customers will go out of their way to accumulate Starwood points by staying in Starwood properties, dining in Starwood restaurants, bringing more visits, more revenues and more profits to Starwood.

Key Learning Point

Anyone who redeems a frequent buyer award has already proven their loyalty to your organization. The experience of 'winning' should make customers eager to come back and win with you again. Remember, what they get from you is not 'free' – they earned it.

Action Steps

Review the procedures for your 'frequent customer program'. Make sure these temporarily 'non-revenue' customers are treated with the high level of special service they deserve: appreciate them, acknowledge them, praise, thank and take good care of them. Remember, ice cream is everywhere and airplane seats are abundant. Giving personal recognition and appreciation through your 'frequent customer program' will ensure that your best customers keep coming back.

Put a CORC in your budget

Alok Kumar is Chief of Operations for a major telecommunications company. In Kumar's business, it takes eight to nine months of revenue to recapture the 'acquisition costs' of each new customer.

Think about that: just to recoup the money spent on advertising, promotion, introductory discounts, new-client administration and data entry requires a customer to remain loyal for eight or nine months! Only after the tenth month does Kumar's company start to reap real profits.

What is the equivalent figure for your company? If you think you make money the very first time your customer buys, think again.

How much money does your company spend attracting new customers?

How much do you spend on retaining existing customers past the crucial tenth month?

In Kumar's case, the answer was shocking! The marketing budget for attracting new customers was huge. But the retention budget for keeping existing customers was tiny. In fact, it wasn't even listed in the budget.

At Kumar's insistence, and only after much effort and experimentation, his company introduced a budget line item called CORC: Cost of Retaining Customers. Starting at 0.8% of revenue, his company carefully tracked results and now dedicates a full 2% of revenue to this new but essential item in the budget.

At first, many people balk at the idea. Why spend money out of profits on customers who are already giving you the profits? Isn't that crazy? Spending exactly the money you've worked so hard to earn?

Not at all! In fact, CORC turns out to be one of the most reliable ways to secure future revenue – into the 12th, 15th and 24th month of customer retention – and profits.

What kind of expenditures go into this CORC line item?

Goodwill gestures when things go wrong are included, but such service-recovery expenses are *reactive* – and are spent only *after* things have gone wrong and customers are upset.

Kumar is more enthusiastic about the *proactive* elements of CORC: sending unexpected gifts to long-term customers, such as surprise bouquets of flowers and dinner vouchers to customers on the tenth month of business. The company even rented an entire movie theatre and filled it with customers and their spouses for a special viewing of a blockbuster movie. Many customers commented that it was the nicest thing any company had done for them in a long time. (And a lot more memorable than just another discount.)

CORC: Cost of Retaining Customers. One of the strongest, smartest and most profitable expense items you'll ever find – or put – in your budget. How big is yours?

Key Learning Point

Spending money on pleasing, surprising and appreciating your existing customers is good business. It keeps them committed to your company and lets them know you value them NOW, not just when they first signed up. Long-term profitability comes from long-term customer retention, not just new customer acquisition.

Action Steps

Figure out how long each customer must be with you before you can recoup your acquisition costs and earn a profit. Then look carefully at how much you spend each subsequent month to *retain* that customer with special activities and efforts.

If your budget is skewed heavily in favor of attracting new customers, but not working hard enough to *keep* them, put a CORC in your budget right away.

Customer discrimination? We do it all the time!

A *Financial Times* editor in London asked my opinion about systems that automatically route customers to higher or lower levels of service based on the loyalty and profitability of the customer.

This happens every day with gold and platinum customers enjoying faster telephone service and shorter lines while everyone else waits and waits.

'Isn't this a case of customer discrimination?' he asked, hoping for a hot topic and response.

My answer was decidedly cool: 'Of course this is customer discrimination. And it is totally appropriate. After all, customers do this with companies all the time.'

The editor was confused until I explained further.

Customers are constantly choosing which companies to patronize, how frequently and with what amount of their available budgets. Companies must do the same: choose which customers to serve, how quickly and with what amount of their available budget.

In both directions, the intention is the same. Customers spend more where they perceive they are getting better service and value. Companies invest more where they see they can obtain better value and long-term 'service' (loyalty) from their customers.

When the matching is done right, it's a win-win situation for both parties. Customers are given an incentive to consolidate their spending, patronage and loyalty behavior with those companies that 'treat them right'. And companies have an incentive to increase their service and special recognition for customers who 'treat them right' with their buying and referral decisions.

What about those who complain and say, 'All companies should give all customers the same service level regardless of how much a customer spends'? To this simplistic and righteous view I reply, 'Wake up and enter the real world. As a customer you insist on your right to choose who to patronize, right? Companies should also have the right to choose which customers they want to attract, retain, cultivate and appreciate.'

Note: This principle may not apply to government services, charitable organizations or companies in a monopoly situation. In these instances, a more uniform level of service may be appropriate.

Key Learning Point

Partnership in business is a two-way street. If you are a customer and want more service from the companies you choose, give them more of your purchases, budget, frequency, constructive input and quality referrals. If you are a company and want more profitable business from the customers you choose, give those customers more of your time, speed, improved systems, well-trained people and other special attention.

Action Steps

As a customer, consolidate your purchasing behavior to reward those companies that serve you well. Don't expect great service if you are not going to be a great customer. For companies, decide which customers you want coming back again and again. Focus your improvements on serving them better over time. Keep your minimum standards up, but save your highest levels of service for those who give you the highest levels of their business.

Long forgotten? Stir old accounts back to life

An award-winning contractor in Savannah, Georgia (who also happens to be my award-winning brother) wrote:

'In my business (home construction and remodeling), I have many accounts with different suppliers supporting the construction industry. Sometimes I use their services and then will not see them again for 8 to 12 months or whenever my next project requires. When I do return to order new supplies, some companies have let my account "run out", and I have to apply for a new account with them all over again.

'I ask why they don't send a card letting me know that my account has become dormant, and is about to be closed? Perhaps they could offer me an incentive to return and make a purchase instead of just "letting me go". After all, they already have me as a good customer, just not very frequent. I just thought this might be happening in other industries as well.'

*   *   *

This is a great question, and a terrific point for anyone seeking to grow their business. Once a company has the benefit of receiving a customer's business, it makes no sense to close the account simply because the customer has not ordered from you in a while...even a long while. Unless there is substantial cost to keeping an account open, you should allow the customer to return at anytime, and welcome them back with enthusiasm.

Remember, once a customer has purchased from you, they will have become familiar with your products, your location, your ordering system and the way you do business. If they have opened an account, then additional time has been invested in completing paperwork and going through the new-account approval process. This person has now invested time, energy and money in becoming your customer. Why in the world would you be in a hurry to close their account?

Instead of closing the account, take my brother's advice and move in a positive direction. Send dormant accounts a letter asking, 'How are you? We haven't heard from you in a while and we miss you!' Provide an incentive, a discount or other special offer to get these customers back into your business. Put a reasonable expiration date on the offer to encourage prompt response. Let them know you want them back, and that you will appreciate and value their business.

Note: If you must, tell customers their account will go on dormant status by a certain date. But also tell them that reactivating the account will be easy to do whenever they are ready.

You will be amazed at the profitability of your efforts. Customers will be delighted by your show of concern, generosity and attention. Don't assume your customers are 'dead'. Stir them back to life!

Key Learning Point

When accounts go quiet, don't assume the customer is going away. They may be waiting, occupied with something else, or have simply forgotten where you are or how to reach you! One effort at reactivation can make the difference between a customer who comes once and disappears forever, and a customer who comes once, is invited back and stays with you forever.

Action Steps

Identify customers you have not heard from in a while, long enough to be considered dormant, decidedly dull or dead. Now create a simple process to contact these customers and tell them you want them back. Give them an incentive to do business with you in the very near future.

'Pain-in-the-neck' customers

Everyone has customers who complain. Complaining customers tell you what you've done wrong and how you can improve. If you work to keep them happy, they will keep you in business.

That's normal.

But some customers complain and complain and complain. They never stop complaining. No matter what you do, they still complain. If you work too hard to keep these 'pain-in-the-neck' customers happy, they can run you right out of business.

Pain-in-the-neck customers don't want to be satisfied. They like being unsatisfied. They frustrate your staff and irritate your other customers.

Pain-in-the-neck customers are not normal. They are distracting and disturbing. And yet they do exist. (I'll bet you can think of one or two right now.)

So what should you do when a pain-in-the-neck customer complains and complains and complains?

1. Recognize that most complaining customers are *not* a pain in the neck. On average, about 2% of your customer base will complain, but only 2% of that 2% are truly nuts. The rest of your complainers are legitimate customers with specific problems. Solve those problems quickly and you will regain their goodwill and repeat business.

2. If your customer *is* a persistent pain in the neck, your immediate focus should be damage control. Isolate a pain-in-the-neck customer away from your staff, your other customers and your brand.

   One famous theme park uses conveniently located, air-conditioned, pastel-colored rooms first to isolate, and then care for, the occasional pain in the neck. In these rooms, specially trained staff soothe the savage customer with comfortable chairs, cool drinks, healthy snacks and calming music.

Only when pain-in-the-neck customers have regained their sanity are they released back into the park. In the meantime, these disturbing characters are removed from other customers, other staff members and from the colorful theme park itself.

3. When damage control does not work, protect your staff and limit your legal liability. If a pain in the neck uses threats, abusive language or makes potentially harmful gestures, immediately contact Security and let them work it out with your lawyers. That's what Security and legal staff are for. Never let a pain in the neck create an unsafe or dangerous situation.

4. If a pain in the neck is not abusive, but remains persistently unhappy, unpleasant and disruptive, consider passing this special customer to your competition. Maybe they can do a better job.

One airline suffered with a pain in the neck who complained regularly and loudly. After trying to satisfy this person for years, the airline finally sent him a letter:

Dear Mr. Tan,

I understand from crew reports that you have been consistently displeased with the service received on our flights. Please accept my apologies. We are concerned for your happiness every time you travel.

However, as we appear unable to satisfy you despite our best efforts, may I recommend you contact one of the other airlines that flies to your frequent destinations? Attached is a list of telephone numbers for your convenience. Hopefully one of these companies will be more successful in providing the service that you seek.

Of course you are always welcome on our flights. And should you choose to fly with us again and enjoy the level of service we do provide, we will be happy to welcome you back on board.

Sincerely,

Senior Manager of Customer Affairs

5. Finally, and most importantly, don't let pain-in-the-neck customers take what they really want from you – which is more and more (and even more!) of your precious time and attention.

Note: Government organizations may not have the option of passing on pain-in-the-neck customers to another organization. In fact, to do so could amplify the problem. When a pain in the neck appears at a government counter, simply draw a line and limit the time.

Key Learning Point

If a pain-in-the-neck customer throws a tantrum on your floor, do what you can to appease him, but if necessary, show him the door.

Action Steps

Review this principle with your managers and staff. Let everyone rant for two minutes about your pain-in-the-neck customers. (Everyone knows who they are.) Then stop wasting your time. Limit the attention you give away (getting nothing in return). Decide what you will and *will not* do when a pain in the neck keeps complaining.

Don't fire your customers! Try upgrading them first

All over the world I teach people how to serve, surprise and delight their customers – how to keep them coming back for more.

But once in a while a client asks, 'Should we keep every customer, no matter what they do, or what they cost?'

My answer: Absolutely not!

Some paying customers cost more to keep than they contribute to your bottom line. Perhaps they cost too much to acquire in the first place. Or they prove too expensive to care for over time. They might purchase the minimum while extracting the maximum from your systems and your staff.

There may be nothing malicious about these people. They are simply unprofitable customers.

Your first approach should be to *upgrade* these patrons to become more valuable customers.

For example, you might impose an administrative fee on below-minimum balances. But if your customers increase their volume, you agree to waive the fee.

You could offer no-charge delivery for orders over a certain amount, but impose a shipping and handling charge for small (and otherwise unprofitable) orders.

You might provide bare-bones service to customers who rarely visit or only purchase a small amount. But if these customers come more frequently or spend more money, you can agree to enhance the service they receive.

This is a constructive win-win approach to an otherwise win-lose situation.

But be careful! Implementing this strategy requires carefully and well-planned scripted communication with your customers *before* you make the change. Present the upgrade path as an opportunity to get more benefits and greater value, not as a penalty for their low-volume business.

But what should you do with customers who choose *not* to increase their business with you? Easy. Either charge them enough that they become profitable to keep, or guide them to alternative service providers who can meet their needs and budget.

Note: There are special cases where this 'upgrade' approach should *not* be applied.

1. Unprofitable customers may be related to very profitable customers, and hence quite sensible to keep. For example, small children might buy very little, but their grandparents might buy *them* quite a lot!

2. Government agencies may be required by law to serve everyone equally. Public charities may not even track the cost of service from one individual to the next.

3. Your company might serve low-income customers regardless of their profitability as a social contribution and valuable community service.

Key Learning Point

Unprofitable customers are just waiting to help you make a profit. What are they waiting for? An attractive offer to upgrade – from you!

Action Steps

Figure out which customers cost more to serve than they generate in profits. Decide how much more you want them to spend, and how much more you are able to give for it. Extend an invitation and seek their increased business. Let them know what they will receive and what they must give for this win-win exchange of service.

What do you think? Will you always go the extra mile?

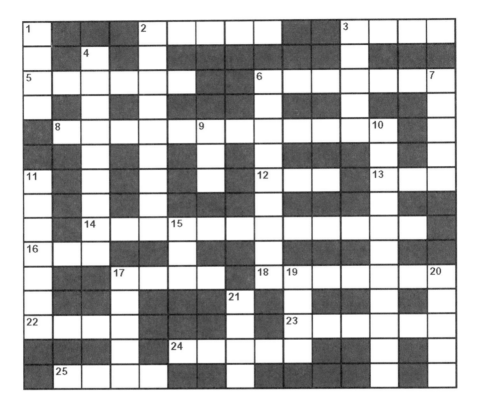

Answers in the Appendix...but don't look yet. Keep trying!

Puzzle clues

Across

2	To give or do something
3	Beyond or previous
5	Gaps
6	True, authentic
8	Customized for a particular person
12	Include some more
13	Give money for services rendered
14	Showing interest and energy
16	Start of many queries
17	Put a value on
18	Hug of appreciation
22	'The customer is ____'
23	Moving with great speed to an objective
24	Predictable sequence of events
25	Express one's choice

Down

1	Force or urge
2	Failure to notice
3	Stop for a limited time
4	Put by for a rainy day! (2 words)
6	Charge and motivate the sales team
7	Relax and ____
9	Fresh
10	Creation of an exact copy
11	Connect with people
15	Summer months are popular?
17	In the ____ place, at the proper time
19	Additional
20	Always enthusiastic
21	Pleasant, kind

CHAPTER

5

PEOPLE MAKE THE DIFFERENCE

What's the difference that makes the difference?
It's the people (of course)!

Empowerment makes dollars and sense

Empowerment exists when employees have the authority to make decisions and take appropriate actions without first seeking approval from others. Empowerment allows frontline service staff to act quickly for their customers, improving customer satisfaction and boosting staff morale.

Brendan sent this example:

'I use an internet grocery delivery in London called Ocado. I'm impressed with this company for the design of their website, the friendliness of the delivery staff, commitment to a one-hour delivery window and much more! *Everything* is designed for what the customer wants, not what is easy for the company. They get a lot of repeat business from me and my friends.

'Recently, Ocado substituted an item, a standard practice when something I order is not available. I did not notice the substitution at the time of delivery (although Ocado usually makes it clear when they have done this).

'When the next delivery arrived, I asked to return the item (worth 5 pounds) for a refund. The delivery person immediately took 5 pounds off my bill and then said, "You know what, you can keep the item anyway."

'The driver didn't have to call anyone else to ask if he could do this, he just did it. Terrific! The company empowers him and trusts him to look after their customers right at the doorstep. Ocado will earn those 5 pounds from me many times over.'

Empowering the delivery person gives the customer what he or she wants *and* is best for the company, too. Imagine the administrative costs of processing a refund claim, bringing a product back to the warehouse, restocking the shelf, adjusting the inventory, etc. All that effort for an item of such low value! Yet that's exactly what most grocery stores around the world would do.

Grocery is a low-margin business. The best, fastest and most intelligent thing to do is what the driver did: turn a low-value item into a high-value customer moment.

Key Learning Point

Empowerment works for your customers, your staff and your organization. Customers get what they need done quickly and done right. The staff becomes more positive and professional. Your organization earns a reputation (and loyal customers) no amount of advertising can buy.

Action Steps

Ask your frontline staff what they *cannot* do for customers without first getting a manager's approval. Now ask yourself what you might gain if staff could act immediately. If there are credit risks or financial limits involved, set them high enough to be worth the time and effort your administrative procedures will require. Otherwise, let your service team do what's right – right away.

'I want to speak to a supervisor!'

A young man working for a Big Boss made an expensive mistake his first week on the job. At the end of the week the young man cleaned out his desk and packed up his things to leave.

The big boss asked, 'And just what do you think you are doing now?'

'I'm leaving,' said the young man. 'I made such an expensive mistake, surely you don't want me to come back here again next week.'

'Are you kidding?' exclaimed the Big Boss. 'I just spent a small fortune educating you. You'd better come back next week and show me what you learned.'

(Does this makes sense to you? If so, read on...)

＊　＊　＊

Have you ever asked a frontline service provider for something special and been told, 'Sorry, company policy. The answer is NO!'

Have you ever asked to speak with the supervisor and found the answer soon changed to YES?

When this happens (and it does all over the world) how do you feel about the company? Do you respect the organization more, or less?

How do you feel about the supervisor? Do you admire their use of authority, or feel pity for the frontline staff they overrule?

How do you think the frontline service provider feels? (And whose rule was he following in the first place when he said, 'The answer is NO.'?)

One supervisor took this problem a step further and asked me the following question:

Dear Ron,

In our business, customers who get special treatment come back later and they only want to speak with a supervisor and no one else. These customers have lots of friends and tell everybody. I am afraid everyone will want the same special treatment.

In the end we would have no need for counter clerks as the supervisors would be serving all our customers! This might make the customers happy, and that is our ultimate goal, but it would be too much for our supervisors to handle. We have plenty of other work to do! How can we solve this situation?

Here is my answer:

Companies should empower frontline staff to do what the supervisor ultimately does, without having to check with the supervisor each and every time. This means staff must get training to *know* what's right – and have authority to *do* what's right.

It means supervisors must trust their staff to do the right thing at the right time and not abuse the privilege. It also means frontline staff must learn the skills required – and earn the trust desired.

This approach shifts the supervisor into the role of educator and motivator rather than controller and dominator. It's a huge change of mindset and culture in any organization.

And it's the right thing to do for two reasons:

One: The experience customers have with your company must be positive and uplifting, or they won't come back. If your customer must get in touch with a supervisor to get satisfaction, more flexible competitors may take your customer away.

If, however, you can please your customers, inspire your customers, and make your customers feel welcome in a non-bureaucratic way, their desire to come back (and tell others) will grow.

This is essential for successful business in today's fast-changing and customer-centric world.

Two: The cost of staff doing robotic work (and referring every exception to the supervisor) is simply too high to sustain. Companies that invest wisely in appropriate training will do far better than those who overspend on high levels of supervisory staff.

Customers get smarter every day. So smart companies provide self-service tools for most basic needs. Well-trained frontline staff should spend their time helping new customers get acquainted and assisting repeat customers with any special situations.

This makes sense, and it makes money.

The next time you need to go beyond the frontline staff to get what you want from a supervisor, ask yourself this question: 'Would you rather go to another business if the staff in that organization could say "yes" to you in the first place?'

If so, let the first business know. And if they still won't empower their staff, then get up and go!

Key Learning Point

Give your frontline team the training and authority they need to take care of customers without constantly asking for approval. This will help you build your business, please your customers and keep your most able staff loyal and growing.

Action Steps

Make a complete list of everything your frontline staff *cannot* do for customers without getting a supervisor's permission. (Hint: ask your frontline staff to make the list.)

Now scrutinize the items one by one and do everything you can to make the list simpler and shorter. Where staff can be trained to decide for themselves, train them. Where guidelines are needed, provide them. If mistakes will be made, allow for them. Over time, everyone can learn to do what only the supervisor used to do.

Empowerment is simple, really. Give good staff the authority to make a decision and tell them to use their common sense. If they bring a situation to you that they should handle themselves, turn it back to them. If they make a good decision, pat them on the back. If they make a bad decision, pat them on the back for doing *something* and then help everyone learn from the mistake.

One more thing: Leaving things as they are is *not* an option for success. Your best staff will leave in frustration, your customers will leave for better service elsewhere, and you will be right where you were at the beginning, making all the decisions...alone.

'I want to speak to a supervisor!' – Part 2

In my regular newsletter, I pointed out how companies should empower and support frontline staff to do what the supervisor ultimately does, without having to check with the supervisor each and every time.

Many readers sent in follow-up questions and suggestions.

* * *

Question: 'If we do give staff more power, how can we measure if it is properly utilized?'

Ron's reply:

You should measure utilization of empowerment only by counting returning customer visits or resulting customer compliments. If your high-value customers come back, make new purchases or praise your service, then your staff empowerment policy is effective.

However, if high-value customers do not praise and come back, or if only low-value customers are happy and re-turning, then you need to change your staff empowerment formula.

Here's a hint: Contact some of your high-value customers who did *not* return. Ask them *why* they didn't come back – and what your staff should have done to earn their repeat visit. Listen carefully. Your former customers will tell you exactly what to do.

And here's an added bonus: Just asking 'non-returning cus-tomers' what it would take to get them back – very often gets them back! Sometimes it's not money that counts, but your time and personal attention.

* * *

Question: 'How do we know where to set limits so the liability of additional cost are minimized?'

Ron's reply:

To limit your liability, put a simple cap on expenditures allowed without supervisor approval. Be sure to link the financial cap to actual client value. Small clients, small cap. Big clients with big budgets, larger amounts allowed. Test this over time to get the right mix of flexibility and generosity by tracking your clients' reactions.

Remember, the ultimate deciding factor is whether good clients return and how much they are worth to your business with their repeat purchases and referrals. As long as customers come back, buy more and refer others, your expense is not a liability, it's a smart investment.

*   *   *

Ken Orr, a Hotel Manager in New Zealand, wrote:

After many long meetings to discuss our customer service levels, we came to a standstill. Supervisors and managers alike insisted they were doing all they could with the frontline staff we have. Every time the frontliners had an issue, I had to come to the rescue.

We knuckled down to find a solution. An 'empowerment pad' was our answer. Each frontline staff member now carries one of these pads and when they see or hear of an issue in our hotel they note down the problem, quickly solve it and then pass on the docket for future consultation.

We provided solutions to all the issues we could think of and told the frontliners to seek and destroy all of our remaining customer-frustrating and lack-of-empowerment issues.

The staff are visibly more vibrant and do not fear the situations they get into with our clients; they are now *looking* for potential problems and pre-empting the solutions! Our supervisors are relaxed and they are now encouraging and motivating the staff like never before.

I have read your newsletter to all my staff. Thank you for a perfectly timed lesson in customer service. Our organization is moving upward; it is very exhilarating.

Thanks, again! Ken Orr

Ken's got the right idea – and is enjoying the right results. You can do this with your team, too!

*   *   *

Question: 'If the frontline staff is not actually our own staff, but belong to an authorized distributor or service center (independent entities), can we apply the same principle?'

Ron's reply:

Yes! I believe the *same* principle can apply and even become the foundation for stronger collaboration between you and your authorized 'Service Partners'. When you show trust by allowing distributors and licensees to make real decisions with real dollars for real customers, they will feel your real appreciation and respect.

That can make your company stand out from all the other companies whose products they also distribute, and can also lead to active word-of-mouth recommendations for you. A real win-win.

Key Learning Point

Empowerment is intelligent fuel for creating self-motivated staff who will love the customers, love their jobs – and love working with you!

Action Steps

Make 'empowerment' your topic of the month. Get everyone involved. Give frontline staff all the empowerment you can imagine, and then try giving a little bit more. The risks are low, the learning value is high and the benefits are truly rewarding.

Responsibility + Sensitivity = Cooperative Authority

E.J. wrote from the Middle East:

> Ron, I was wondering if you can give me some advice. I work as a salesman and the company owner is a DICTATOR. Nothing is accepted unless he personally approves it. That's causing us big problems since we can't sell on the spot. And if the bargain isn't completed at the moment, someone else will come and take it. Salesmen here don't have any authority to do anything. We get embarrassed in front of our clients. This is not professional. And if anyone talks about this problem, the owner simply says, 'It's my money and not yours.' What can I do to convince him? I would appreciate your ideas about this.

*   *   *

Excellent question, E.J. Here's my reply:

Sometimes business owners and department heads can be very restrictive. Sometimes it is due to insecurity, sometimes to past bad experiences, sometimes they are simply unsure how to loosen the reins.

One course of action you can take is to give your company owner a *proposal* outlining the exact situations you are concerned about, and the parameters you would like to be able to approve on the spot for your clients.

Make the guidelines conservative (at first) so you can be

reasonably sure he will approve your initial request. Such a proposal would get things going in the right direction and give you some (although very limited) freedom.

Work within this approved range for a couple of weeks or months, still going back to him as agreed (and with a smile) for personal approval of everything else.

After some time has passed and he can see you are following the rules, ask him to stretch the range just a bit more, and then a bit more, and then...you get the idea.

The key is not to fight him, push him or even complain about him! Rather, work with him to create a clear protocol and build up his comfort and confidence first. Ask for more later.

EM-POWER-ment will come more quickly when you demonstrate EMpathy as well as your eagerness for POWER.

Key Learning Point

Empowerment is essential for any growing business, and certainly for growing careers. To gain more authority, take more responsibility and show more sensitivity. That's being responsible, too.

Action Steps

If you are stuck in a situation where you have little leeway, finite freedom or just a dribble of discretion, use this approach to improve things s-l-o-w-l-y but surely.

Passionate for continuous learning

I am sometimes asked, 'Where did you go to school and what did you study?'

I graduated from Brown University in 1979 with a degree in International Political History. But my education only began there.

In the years since graduation, I have continued learning through a wide range of personal and professional workshops. Here are a few of the highlights:

I attended The Sage Experience with Brandon Saint John, est by Werner Erhard, the Loving Relationships Training with Sondra Ray, DMA (based on *The Path of Least Resistance* by Robert Fritz) and The Seven Habits Course by Steven Covey.

I participated in the Hoffman Quadrinity Process, the Landmark Forum and their Advanced Course, and three courses of Harry Palmer's Avatar training in Asia, Europe and the United States.

I became a licensed bodywork therapist in Sacramento, studied leadership with Marshall Thurber, conscious breath work with Leonard Orr, neurolinguistics with Tony Robbins, Rich Dad Investing with Robert Kiyosaki, internet marketing with Tom Antion and Wealth Dynamics with Roger Hamilton.

I was a client for three months with Dale Carnegie, eight months with *E-Myth* author Michael Gerber, studied one year in Peter Montoya's Personal Branding University and five glorious years in the Ontological Design Course with Dr. Fernando Flores.

I've attended industry conferences in training and customer service, conventions and workshops in professional speaking and listened to countless recordings of keynote presentations, single-topic seminars and weekend workshops.

Even today I continue to learn through coaching sessions in presentation skills, public relations, business planning and website design – and through active participation in three different communities of personal and professional learning.

I don't tell you this to brag or to confirm your suspicion that I am still very much a 'work in progress'. Rather, I seek to encourage *you* to be absolutely passionate in *your life* for a wide-ranging course of ambitious, continuous and enthusiastic learning.

Whether through books, tapes, coaching and classes, seminars, workshops or conventions, personal reflection or shared exploration, *now* is the time to keep your mind alert, your body growing, your heart wide open and your horizons of life expanding.

Key Learning Point

The passionate pursuit of continuous learning is an essential element for your continued success.

Action Steps

Commit today to learn something new, or something more, to keep yourself moving forward. It can be growth stocks or gardening, technical skills or tantra, relationships or real estate, negotiations, neural networks or knitting. Whatever it is and however you do it, *take action* to keep on learning!

Are you a real professional?

The customer was just leaving the service counter and said to the young man who had helped her, 'You are a real professional. Thank you.'

The young man blushed. To be called 'a real professional' is a very powerful compliment. It's not easy to achieve. Real professionals perform well in five key areas:

1. **Knowledge:** Real professionals understand what other people want and need, what their own products and services can provide, where and how to get assistance, what's changing in their own company and in the world of those they serve. How good is your product, process, service and industry knowledge? Want to improve? Read more, listen better, discuss with others, get mentoring, get coaching, get going.

2. **Skills:** Real professionals are proficient and skillful. They know how to do the right thing at the right time and in the right way. How good are your hard skills (technical competence) and soft skills (getting things done with people)? Need to improve? Study and practice new techniques, watch the masters in action, get more training, get more qualified. Be really good, then get better.

3. **Attitude:** Real professionals are more than technically bright. Their enthusiasm is motivating and infectious. Customers feel assured by their confidence. Colleagues are touched by their compassion. How powerful is your attitude? Need to improve? Get clear about what turns you on and why you care to serve. Align your values with your company's goals, your customers' needs and your colleagues' shared commitment. And watch your mindset like a hawk. No whining when you should be shining.

4. **Effort:** Real professionals have a strong will and ambition to succeed. They may be humble, but they are not shy about striving for spectacular performance. These winners go the extra mile and help others along the way. They push themselves and drive their teams to greater achievement. And customers reinforce their effort with well-earned praise. How strong is your effort? Want to increase it? Then set big, bold goals and high, stretching targets. Do something every day to move on, move up, move forward.

5. **Relationships:** The greatest professionals help other people move into the future. They make suggestions to solve your immediate problem and then give guidance to take you further. They anticipate your questions and prepare answers in advance. They think about *your* success and give advice that's packed with value. Want to strengthen your relationships with others? Learn to listen more closely for real concerns. Make offers without being asked. Network with others in your company, your industry, your town. Lend a hand whenever you can and be willing to receive one.

Key Learning Point

Real professionals are well-rounded in their ability, approach and actions. They are always improving, uplifting themselves and motivating those around them.

Action Steps

Study the above five areas closely. Choose one that needs your attention. Now commit to take a strong step forward. What will you do? Who will you call? Where can you get help? Get started. Make it happen. Then give yourself the credit you deserve. You are 'a real professional'.

New titles open new possibilities

In my writing I've pointed out how titles can influence the moods and expectations of those around us.

Here are some good examples sent in from readers around the world:

'We changed our Human Resources Department to Department for People Support.'

'We use "Partner-In-Charge of..." whatever area someone has. It makes us all feel equal in a flat organization. We just changed the Office Manager to "Partner-In-Charge of Customer Delight".'

'My job responsibilities include project manager, business development manager and senior consultant. Ah, where's the customer? So I've changed my title to "Value Creation Consultant".'

The Product and Sales Manager at my book distributor changed his own title to 'Author Champion'.

My titles have included author, speaker, trainer, consultant and curriculum developer. I've stopped trying to name my position. Now I just relate the mission: 'Leading the Global Service Revolution!'

Key Learning Point

What you call yourself and your colleagues has a big effect on how people understand who you are, what you do and how you can assist. Choose a title that opens the door and connects with other people.

Action Steps

You can change your title, too. (Should you?)

Dead wood: high value antiques or dangerous rot?

Every organization must reckon with 'old-timers': staff who have served many years but may be past their most productive prime.

What should you do with these folks?

Firing them seems a mercenary way to run a business. But keeping them on staff can demotivate and demoralize others, increasing your payroll without improving profits.

A journalist recently asked me point-blank, 'What should companies do with their "dead wood"?'

My answer was a question; 'Is the "dead wood" raw material for valuable antiques, or is it dangerous rot?'

Many long-serving staff have a wealth of experience, customer knowledge and good ideas. They can be valuable in training new staff, contacting and caring for customers, spreading goodwill for the company through public relations or community outreach programs.

Long-serving staff may not be able to master the latest technology or move at the current pace of change, but their knowledge and proven skills could still be harnessed for the benefit of all. These team members are raw material for creating treasured and high-value antiques.

One large company offered senior staff an option of retiring early or working in new capacities as recruiters, staff trainers or customer service personnel. Each of these positions offered a lower level of salary but recognized and leveraged the staff members' years of experience. Half of those offered the new positions stayed on, adding new value to the organization. The other half moved on.

Another company offered no salary at all, but provided office facilities and a generous incentive program so that older staff could contact former customers to help stimulate or reactivate their accounts.

The success rate was tremendous.

Each conversation brought together a long-serving staff member with a long-standing (but no longer active) customer. Rapport was easily established as both sides shared experiences and insights about the company, its services and products. Many of these heart-to-heart conversations resulted in reactivation of accounts, new purchases, new profits and plenty of new ideas for the company.

From old wood came precious antiques.

But what about long-serving staff who have become cynical, resentful and demoralized? What about those who speak badly about the company and complain openly to customers and other staff?

These employees are toxic and contagious. They are the unhealthy rot that can destroy the competitiveness and the culture of your organization. Such 'rotten apples' should be excised as quickly and cleanly as possible. To keep them around through some misguided interpretation of loyalty is sheer lunacy.

If someone is earning money from an organization, they owe their active loyalty to the current health and future well-being of that organization – period.

Two points to note: (warning – may be controversial)

1. The commercial world is changing too fast for inflexible employment entitlements. Union agreements that arrest or retard an industry's ability to innovate are doing an injustice to the industry, the companies and the countries in which they work. Short-term gains for a few may result in long-term losses for everyone.

2. Everyone in an organization should add value or be released. Pay should be based on value contributed to the organization in current time – not on continuous recognition of value generated in the past.

Old-timers may not be able to generate the same amount of sales value or productivity as before, and their compensation could be adjusted accordingly.

But given the option of working in new ways, creating new value and earning a new (sometimes lower) income, many staff will choose that route over leaving employment altogether.

Key Learning Point

As the population and workforce age, many companies can benefit by taking an innovative approach to keeping their long-serving members on staff. This plan for creating and delivering new value should be initiated early so that old wood can be transformed into beautiful and valuable antiques...before it rots.

Action Steps

Review how your organization currently harnesses the experience of your longest-serving staff. Create a focus group of current and former employees, customers and suppliers to brainstorm together. Find new ways for old-timers to create new value for the future.

Do the one BIG thing

Ever procrastinate? Who doesn't!

I often find myself digging through piles of mail, e-mail, invoices, newspapers and telephone messages when something more important is waiting for my attention.

The thought of that 'one BIG thing' weighs on my mind, gnawing at my sense of peace and calm.

Writing it on my 'to-do list' doesn't help. Only doing it gets it done. And oh! – the surge of energy and relief that accompanies completion!

___

Key Learning Point

When you stop procrastinating and start doing, you release the energy you need to get other things done. (You feel better, too.)

___

Action Steps

This month, pick 'one BIG thing' to improve the service you provide. Choose one big thing you've known about for some time – one that sits in the back of *your* mind, gnawing away at your peace and calm.

Maybe it's updating your website, revising a procedure, creating a customer appreciation campaign. Perhaps it's upgrading your skills, teaching your team, resolving issues that need attention.

Whatever it is: you know what it is. It's the one BIG thing that needs you. These things must be done eventually. Make eventually today.

Take this test and see: How much difference do you make?

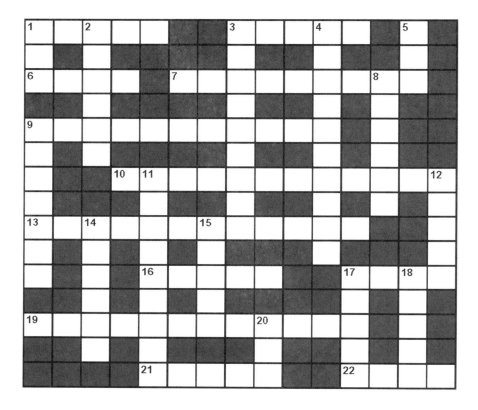

Answers in the Appendix. But you've got all the answers already, right?

Puzzle clues

Across

1 Make a formal request
3 Be quick in completing the task
6 Appointment; tropical fruit
7 A standard against which to measure good service
9 From one country to another (2 words)
10 In harmony (hyph.)
13 Easy for consumers to understand and operate (hyph.)
16 A difficult customer can make you ____ !
17 The highest level that one can reach
19 Customer satisfaction network (2 words)
21 Businesses can only ____ with customer loyalty
22 Exchange goods or services for money

Down

1 Total up
2 Supporter
3 Having high moral standards
4 Unusual and worth noticing
5 Request information
8 Decrease
9 Behavior or approach
11 Achieving the intended result
12 Lack of certainty
14 Check
15 Enraged
17 Extra payment or benefit
18 ____ a rat
20 Popular, among the cool!

CHAPTER

6

BUILD YOUR
SERVICE CULTURE

Building a strong service culture is a big job. With careful planning and these great ideas, you can get it done!

Get new staff to 'self-select'

If you want a strong and distinctive company culture, you need to get the *right* people on the job.

If you want innovation, hire creative people. If you want aggressive sales results, hire those with an energized 'can-do' attitude. If you want to give great customer service, only hire people who will go the extra mile.

But how can you find such people in a market filled with so many resumes, retrenchments and retirees? How can you avoid wasting time and money hiring new staff, only discovering later they weren't the right people for the job?

Well-designed job interviews can be useful; candid referrals may help. Personality profiles may also reveal who a person really is, and isn't.

But here's another approach that will save you time and money, though it is very rarely used: raise the bar during the recruitment process so job seekers 'self-select'.

You want innovation? Run your recruitment advertisement *upside down* in the newspaper. (It will be the only one, and will definitely stand out!) Ask interested applicants to provide specific examples of how *they* do things 'differently' (and better) in their lives and in their work.

You want ambitious, aggressive sales staff? Arrange job interviews at one location, then leave a note taped on the door explaining that the location has been changed at the last minute to somewhere else. Include a short apology and a map, and request those still interested to come to a different building several blocks away. At the new location, leave another note, this time moving the meeting down the hall or up a few flights of stairs.

Now interview and select only those applicants who arrive *energized* by this process. Those who complain, are

BUILD YOUR SERVICE CULTURE

upset or exhausted won't have the stamina to chase down sales leads and succeed.

You want to hire people who truly believe in great customer service? Conduct job interviews at 8:00 pm on a Friday night. When applicants arrive, ask them to help you pack a last-minute customer order before the interview begins. Then have someone call in (pre-arranged) pretending to be your customer. Help them patiently over the phone, delaying your interview by a few more minutes. Watch your applicant's mood throughout this process. Hire only those who smile and nod with understanding as they see *you* giving extra-mile service.

The MGM Hotel in Las Vegas applied this approach in a fast and effective manner. They needed to hire hundreds of new staff in a short period of time, but thousands of job seekers applied. One-by-one the applicants were guided down a long hallway. As they approached a junction at the end of the hall, an MGM recruiter looked up from his desk and said in a plain tone of voice, 'Hello.'

Applicants who responded with clear eye-contact, a warm smile and a positive tone were guided to the right side for immediate interviews and job offers. Those who responded with a blank stare or a flat tone of voice were gently guided to the left side – and out the door.

Key Learning Point

It's important to get the right people into your organization, and it's expensive to hire the wrong ones. Be creative with your recruitment and interview process. Take time at the start to help your best job applicants 'self-select'.

Action Steps

Look closely at your current recruitment and interviewing process. Does it identify job applicants who are truly aligned with your mission, values and culture? How can you change, improve or modify the process to quickly attract those you want, and easily decline those you don't?

It pays to help new staff start right

Effectively orienting your new employees can pay big dividends in staff retention, employee commitment, company culture and customer satisfaction.

Staff members who are properly trained and welcomed at the beginning of their careers will feel good about their choice of employer, fit in more quickly with peers and colleagues and readily contribute new ideas.

Properly oriented employees will also speak well about your organization to their family and friends. They will represent you more confidently with customers, business partners and suppliers.

But poor orientation of new employees can cost you dearly.

Those who don't start right don't tend to stay long, either. High staff turnover means you must recruit, hire, orient and train new staff all over again.

Staff turnover also takes a high toll on the morale of those who remain behind. When people leave your organization, those who remain inevitably wonder if they should seek new employment, too.

While many managers agree that orientation is important, very few invest the time and attention necessary to make sure it's done right *and* consistently. *Now* is a good time to review your staff orientation program to be sure *your* new staff 'start right'.

Here are some guidelines to doing it right:

Think long-term.

Effective orientation is a gradual process and does not end after the second day on the job. The initial induction of employees during the first few days is important. But it is even more important to make sure new employees fit in and feel comfortable over the long term. This can mean six weeks for a factory worker, or up to six months for new members of a senior management team.

A time for everything, everything in it's time.

New employees arrive with basic questions that must be answered quickly: 'What is the dress code? Where are the tools for my job? How does the telephone system work? When do people eat, meet and get paid?'

After the initial induction period, your employee's questions will change and mature: 'How am I being appraised? Why is the system set up this way? How can I (safely) suggest changes? Who can I see for guidance, approval and support?'

Don't try to answer all possible questions in the least possible time. Stretch out the process to cover the first weeks or months on the job. This lets new staff understand essential information more gradually – and thus more completely.

An extended orientation program also reassures new employees. Newcomers are under great pressure to perform and adapt. Your extended program shows you understand their situation, you care about their adjustment and you will continue to show interest and support over time.

Involve everyone in the process.

New employees are not the only ones affected by the design and quality of your orientation program. Other groups are influenced during this important period as well: peers, bosses, junior staff, senior managers, customers, suppliers and even the new hire's family back home.

Each group has different questions and concerns about the new employee. You can address their concerns by giving these groups an active role in the overall orientation program. Buddy systems, lunch meetings, panel discussions, site visits, family days – these methods and other activities can involve diverse groups of individuals in the overall orientation process.

The reputation of your human resources and training departments are also at stake. If orientation is well planned and conducted, these departments will be seen by new employees as a valuable resource for addressing their future concerns. On the other hand, poor staff orientation sends an early message that these 'people departments' are ineffective or out-of-touch.

A well-designed orientation program should accomplish seven major objectives:

1. Create comfort and rapport.

Newcomers want to feel a sense of acceptance and belonging inside their new organization. You can accelerate this process by creating abundant opportunities for new hires to interact with peers, managers, direct reports, colleagues from other departments, customers and suppliers.

Diversify the time and nature of these meetings. Coffee breaks, meal times and after-hours get-togethers are all good choices for informal conversations. Include new hires in formal gatherings as well: customer visits, focus groups and even department or management meetings.

Send your new employees on short assignments to visit other divisions and departments. Spending a week, a day or even an afternoon in a different part of the business will do wonders to build rapport and understanding for the new hires throughout your organization.

2. Introduce the company culture.

New staff usually want to fit in with accepted norms and values. 'How do things *really* work around here? What importance do people attach to style, dress, presentation? Is punctuality important? Do meetings start on time? Are long hours the exception or expected?'

Understanding the company culture only comes over time, through formal presentations, informal dialogue and a lot of personal experience. What gets said 'officially' is compared with what gets said 'confidentially' during lunch, after hours and between colleagues in the washroom.

Extend your positive influence beyond the formal presentations. Create a buddy system or mentor program to match your most successful and enthusiastic staff with your incoming employees.

But don't expect your enthusiastic staff to stay that way if their mentor role becomes a burden. Give the mentor relationship real support: pay for lunches, allow time in the work schedule for mentoring conversations, include mentoring in your annual staff appraisal and show genuine appreciation to your chosen mentors with tokens of reward, recognition and respect.

3. Showcase the 'Big Picture'.

You must help new staff find honest answers to all of the following questions:

'Where has this company been? Where is it today? Where are we heading tomorrow? Who are our customers? What do they say about us? Who are our major competitors? What is our market position?

'What is our current focus? Are we expanding operations, going regional and launching new technologies? Or are we trimming costs, stabilizing product lines and streamlining operations?'

You can orient new staff to these 'big picture' issues with a well-designed presentation. Using multi-media, highlight your history and present status, future targets, goals and directions. Share humble beginnings, detail greatest achievements.

Show excitement for future direction, but be candid about company weaknesses, too. Talk openly about difficulties and challenges in the market. Keep your 'big picture' presentation lively and up-to-date.

In large organizations, very senior managers are often the best authorities to share insights on the future of the business. But these same managers may frequently be out of town or involved in handling current situations. They are not always available when you want them to participate in a new staff orientation session.

You can solve this problem by capturing them on video as they discuss the opportunities and challenges facing your organization. Then use the video in your program and bring the managers back 'live' at a later date for panel discussions, question-and-answer sessions or informal 'meet the manager' conversations.

4. Explain job responsibilities and rewards.

Clearly define your expectations from the beginning. Ensure new staff are well versed in their responsibilities and corresponding levels of authority.

Demonstrate and thoroughly explain your approach to staff appraisal. Show new staff the actual appraisal system and illustrate how good performance will be measured, assessed and rewarded.

Point to the career paths of those who have come before to illustrate advancement possibilities and potential.

5. Handle administrative matters.

There will always be detailed procedures to follow and paperwork or online procedures to complete: employment agreements, insurance policies, benefits packages, charitable contribution forms, locker allocation, issuing passwords, uniform distribution – the list goes on and on.

While these are important, resist the temptation to 'get it all over with' in one long (and very boring) session.

Instead, spread those administrative tasks over several short sessions in the first few weeks. Hours spent filling out forms on the first day at work is *not* the way to inspire enthusiasm about the dynamic nature of your organization!

6. Provide reality checks.

Make sure your orientation program is not a fantasy tour of what you wish the company would be.

If your program shows only the bright side of the business and the happy side of daily work, don't be surprised if new employees are shell-shocked after two or three weeks on the job.

Be open and candid about the pressures and realities of your company, your team, your customers, your industry and your competition.

One large regional firm developed an extensive orientation program along the following theme: 'You will know more about the problems of this organization than the people who have worked here for years!'

This novel approach creates new staff who understand the realities and are ready to work – and work hard – to help their company succeed.

7. Gain full participation.

Give everyone a role to play in new employee orientation. Involve peers and colleagues in your mentor programs and buddy teams; engage top managers in talks and panel discussions; give junior staff a stake as hosts and guides in cross-department visits.

Invite the new staff's family members to a special 'Meet the Company Day' and take photographs at the event. Later, send the best photos back to their homes with a copy of your company's newsletter – and a handwritten note from *you* to the entire family.

Most important of all, gain full participation from the new employees themselves. Resist the temptation to project all the information in a one-way stream from the company to the new staff. Have your newcomers explore the company, research the competition, meet the customers – and then generate their *own* good questions for you and your colleagues to answer.

Finally, get your new employees involved in welcoming the *next* batch of incoming staff. This ensures that your orientation program stays fresh and relevant. It can become a watershed event, making your new staff feel like company veterans: experienced, involved and useful.

Key Learning Point

The time, money and human resources you dedicate to new employee orientation can be one of your best long-term corporate investments. Make sure your program is thoughtfully designed, carefully delivered, continuously upgraded and improved.

Action Steps

Gather a cross-functional team of recent hires, seasoned employees and key managers. Do a complete review of every aspect of your existing new staff orientation program.

How does your current program measure up? What is being done well? What is engaging, motivating and effective? Is anything boring, tedious or out-of-date? What else could be included? What should be taken out?

Revise your program and conduct a trial run. Ask the participants for suggestions to make your program even better. Keep adapting, keep improving. Keep it up!

Make your staff suggestion system make sense

Markets demand greater innovation. Customers have rising expectations. Your competitors are more nimble than ever before.

You need new ideas, efficient processes, innovative products, valuable services, and more effective ways to build a strong future together. Where are you going to get them?

Harness the power of your in-house creative ideas.

Organizations can no longer survive if managers must provide all the answers. Companies need a steady flow of ideas and solutions from those who are closest to the processes and the customers, those with their 'ears to the ground'.

You must develop a culture that actively solicits input and recommendations from *every* level of your staff.

Fortunately, managers are more receptive to this approach than ever before. But how can you transform the mindset of staff who, for years or even generations, were trained to 'keep their mouths shut, lie low and just follow orders'? How can you encourage everyone on your team to open their minds and share their best new ideas?

One technique is the 'staff suggestion system', a time-honored process with pre-printed forms for staff to write their ideas and with wooden boxes on the wall where they submit those ideas for management consideration.

Many companies have tried this, but few can report real satisfaction with the number, consistency or quality of contributions. Even fewer can report widespread enthusiasm for their 'suggestion' schemes at all.

Here are six ideas you can implement right away to make your approach more effective:

1. Respond immediately to all staff suggestions.

Be candid. If the answer is no, say no. If the answer is yes, state when staff will see implementation. If the answer is maybe, explain the issues and give a reliable date for reply.

One exception: Do not reply to obscene or abusive suggestions. A strong company culture has no place for such destructive 'input'. Your best response is not to reply.

2. Respond to suggestions for all to see.

When one person makes a suggestion, she says what is on the minds of many. Reply to suggestions on a bulletin board, in a meeting, or by e-mail to all concerned. Thank the writer for making the contribution.

3. Give prizes for the best suggestions – right away.

Many suggestion programs involve a multi-step process. Suggestions are collected. A committee sorts for 'realistic' submissions. Managers appraise the cost savings and anticipated revenue from each. 'Senior management' decides on the reward to be given. The 'prize' is finally awarded.

The cycle-time for this process is often four weeks or more. In some cases the review is only once a quarter. Would *you* be inspired if you had to wait that long?

Try this approach: Dedicate $1,200 to the project. Give away $100 every month for one year. Each month, give $50 to the best idea, $20 to the second best idea, and $10 each to the next three best suggestions.

In the first month, only a handful of staff may participate. Give out the money anyway. When the staff realizes you are serious, their suggestions will get serious, too.

4. Establish categories for regular awards.

Categories help staff generate new ideas. Try these: ideas that can be implemented immediately, ideas for getting closer to customers, suggestions for cost savings or increasing revenue, ideas focusing on a specific theme, ideas that most dramatically challenge the current way of thinking, recommendations for the future of the business.

5. Prizes deserve publicity.

Make a big event when you give awards. One company uses 'dollar bills' for each winning suggestion. In the center is the the staff member who contributed. In the corners is the amount of money the suggestion earned. Surrounding the portrait is a description of the suggestion itself.

These 'dollar bills' line the walls of the staff lounge and company cafeteria. The result is recognition for winners and a 'culture-building' impact that keeps the suggestion system going strong all year long.

At the end of each year, total the number of suggestions received, acknowledge the winners rewarded and highlight the positive results. Then challenge your team to *double* the volume of suggestions in the coming year. While you're at it, double the volume of rewards.

6. Most important, implement the suggestions quickly.

Act on what your staff suggests. Nothing demonstrates your commitment to this approach better than a staff suggestion recognized, rewarded and immediately put to work.

Are there even more good ways to improve your company's suggestion program? Sure there are. Got a suggestion?

Key Learning Point

It's vital to any company team that they be continually infused with new ideas. Get *your* new ideas from those who are front-and-center. And reap the rewards of inspired employees and innovation!

Action Steps

Attune your staff to a new way of thinking. Develop a strategy that works in your company for a new approach. Maybe someone has a suggestion. If so, grab it and go!

Ban the 'internal customer'

'Internal Customer' is a phrase often heard in business. Usually this refers to one department (the internal customer) receiving work from another department (the internal supplier).

But this phrase has become widespread and is now applied to branch offices, field officers, repair centers, distributors, night shifts, contract workers, parking lot attendants, bosses, employees, job applicants and even retirees.

Motorola has more than one thousand service agents in China repairing and upgrading consumers' mobile phones. Motorola provides spare parts to the service agents, making the agents 'internal customers' of Motorola. But Motorola pays labor fees charged by the service agents under maintenance contracts. So Motorola is also an internal customer of the agents. This could be confusing.

It gets worse when more than two parties are involved, or when people say 'The Customer is King' and then argue over who should be treated more 'royally'!

I think the phrase itself is out-of-date and problematic. Rather than one side taking the 'customer' position and casting the other as 'supplier', both parties could – *and should* – embrace to become 'Internal Service Partners' working together to delight the 'external customer'.

After all, good ideas and extra effort should come from *both* sides in any working relationship. Both 'internal customers' should be committed to creating a positive outcome for their shared 'external customer' down the line.

Within our departments, companies and organizations we are customers and providers to each other.

We are, in truth, service *partners*.

Key Learning Point

The phrase 'internal customer' can lead to awkward attitudes and inappropriate expectations. Replace it with 'internal service partners'.

Action Steps

Get together with those you depend on at work and those who depend on you. Create a shared declaration of service partnership for working effectively together, including listening to each other's concerns, being open to new ideas, sharing insights and new approaches, and making suggestions for improvement.

Keep your service partnership focused on the customer that really counts – the one that makes a choice every day about where to bring their business.

Make the shift from 'me' to 'we'

The most listened-to radio station in the world is WII-FM, which stands for 'What's In It For Me?'

Some people use this question like a trump card. Answer well and you will get my cooperation. If your answer is insufficient I may ignore your question, request or even the entire situation.

I'm tired of this question being used so often and with such depressing power. Here's why:

Little kids go for individual and immediate gratification: 'Give me', 'I want', 'It's mine'.

But we're not little kids anymore, and 'me, me, me' is a pretty narrow place from which to participate in your business and your life.

If you choose a partner then 'you' becomes 'two'. You introduce yourself and say '...and this is my partner, Jenny' or '...this is my husband, Paul.'

If you have a family then 'me' becomes 'we'. You introduce yourself by telling people where you live, what you do for a living and how many children you have.

Your definition of 'me' can be even bigger. If you care deeply about a group, you want *everyone* in the group to succeed. The definition is bigger still if you contribute to an organization, and even bigger if you commit to the well-being of society or take a stand for some change or improvement in the world.

So what's this point of view got to do with you and your work? (I know, I know, 'What's in it for me?')

When you are individually focused ('me, me, me'), it's hard to stand out by giving great service to others. It's easy to slip into being moody, selfish and stingy.

When you make the shift from 'me' to 'we', another person becomes as important *to* you *as* you. His mood counts as much as yours, so you listen more carefully and offer better help. Her needs make a difference in your life, so you pay more attention and do a better job.

When you shift from 'me' to 'we', other people feel taken care of, appreciated and understood. They feel good. And often you feel good, too.

A colleague's good mood brightens up your own. Your customer's satisfaction is part of your success. Your goals get met by helping others reach theirs. 'What's in it for me' is fulfilled by creating what's in it for *them*.

Business is like that. Life is, too. Take a small position and you get a small result. Take a bigger stand for others: more fulfillment and more reward will come right back to you.

Key Learning Point

The common focus on 'me, me, me' prevents people from acting generously toward others. This narrow focus limits what is possible for your business and yourself. To get more of what you want, take a bigger view of who (else) counts and what (else) matters.

Action Steps

Look around where you live and work. Ask yourself: 'Who can I help? Where can I contribute more? How can I play a bigger game?'

If you serve individual customers, make their needs and concerns as important as your own. If you are part of a team, make the team's success your ambition. If you work in a department, work to achieve your department's goals and help other departments achieve theirs, too.

Don't hold back! Contribute more to your customers, colleagues and company. Why bother? What's in it for you? A better way of living – and giving – that fulfills you every day.

No more 'Employee of the Month'!

Do you remember the last time you saw an 'Employee of the Month' award? If you were a customer, did you recognize the name of the winner? Probably not. Could you tell what he or she did to win the award? Unlikely.

If you were a staff member, did someone winning the monthly award motivate you to higher achievements? Doubtful. Did you understand exactly what he or she did to become the monthly winner? More doubtful still.

Awards can stimulate and motivate the staff. But simple 'Employee of the Month' programs can quickly devolve into mindless and political rituals with very little meaning.

You need something more engaging.

Review this list of ideas for meaningful recognition of your staff. Use a different one each month, or several at a time.

Happiest Customer Comment (read it out to everyone)

Most Customers Served (when volume counts)

Best Service Recovery (share the problem, the action *and the outcome*)

Most Effective Service Improvement (What was changed? What was the result?)

Best Internal Service Partner (voted by all *other* staff or departments)

Top Rookie Award (best performance by someone new)

Speedy Service Award (fastest response, repair, delivery or installation)

Terrific Teaching Trophy (for the staff member who helps others learn the most)

Most Supportive Move by the Boss (given by the grateful employees)

Above and Beyond Award (for someone who went the extra mile)

Best Supplier of the Month (bring them in for applause)

Most Valuable Mistake of the Month (What happened? How much did we lose? How much did we learn?)

You can make medals, prizes, trophies, certificates, plaques, ribbons and stars. You can give dinners, cash, time off, flowers or simply abundant applause.

Let people know at the beginning of each month which awards will be granted at the end. Or keep a list of ideas close at hand, and award them spontaneously whenever a winning performance arises. Keep it interesting, keep it fresh, keep it going.

Key Learning Point

People want to work where company culture is dynamic. No more boring 'Employee of the Month'! Create something new and more effective to engage, encourage, focus, motivate, appreciate, stimulate, celebrate and arouse everyone.

Action Steps

Look at the recognition programs you presently apply at work. Are they fresh, interesting and effective? Now make a list of the efforts and actions you want to see *more* of every day: service, sales, cost reductions, work improvement, innovation, teamwork, you name it! Create 'special prizes' for those areas that will inspire your people, improve their performance and enhance your company culture.

Harness the power of praise

'Another day, another dollar', 'Thank God it's Friday', 'You can take this job and shove it!'

Why are so many common phrases about work so negative?

What would it take for *your* people to say: 'Another day, another exciting challenge', 'Thank goodness it's Monday', 'I'll take this job and love it!'?

Some managers claim the best way to motivate staff is through the wallet: increase pay, expand allowances, give more cash incentives. While money is certainly useful, it is not the *only* key to human motivation.

Sincere recognition can mean a lot more to your staff than just another dollar in the bank. A genuine pat on the back, given at the right time, in the right way, for the right reasons – and in front of the right people – will boost staff morale and commitment in ways that money never will.

Openly and honestly thanking each employee for their hard work and dedication can go a long way toward creating a happy and productive team. But don't wait for a special occasion – do it today, and then do it again next week.

What else can you do to build an enduring culture of motivation and reward? What actions can you take to make your people feel recognized, appreciated and esteemed?

Contests and awards do work. But they are not enough to create a challenging and inspirational company culture.

You can make a bigger difference with these four steps to building the long-term morale of your team.

1. Learn from everyone's mistakes.

Before rewarding people for a job well done, assure the

staff that they won't be crucified if things end up poorly. In an environment of challenge and growth, people must try things they've never done before. And they will make mistakes. In a healthy and rewarding culture, people are encouraged to *learn* from their mistakes, and then quickly regroup and rebuild.

Managers should work with employees to understand what went wrong, rectify the situation and then improve the approach. Attack the problem, not the people involved.

Ask your team aloud: 'What can be learned from this mistake? What can be improved? Who else should we inform so they can benefit from the learning, too?'

Many companies have rituals for celebrating success and achievements, and that's good. But it's the mistake no one hears about (and others blindly repeat) that can pull you to the bottom.

'Sweep it under the rug.' 'Turn a blind eye.' 'What they don't know won't hurt them.' These are recipes for disaster.

In *Swim With The Sharks Without Being Eaten Alive*, Harvey McKay writes: 'You'll always get the good news; it's how quickly you get the bad news that counts!'

Reinforce this lesson with your own example. Start your next meeting by sharing the biggest mistake *you've* made in the past two weeks. Explain what you learned from the experience. Then ask others for their ideas, listen to feedback and thank those who offer their opinions.

By taking the lead and sharing your mistakes, you will demonstrate a willingness to learn and encourage a culture of sharing and honest communication.

What about staff who make no mistakes? Either they are very good at hiding what is really going on or they are not being challenged enough. The person who only makes small, safe and bureaucratic moves does not innovate or grow. In today's turbulent markets, this is not what you need to succeed.

2. Make appraisal criteria clear.

Make sure the staff understands how they will be appraised for raises, bonuses and promotions. Whether you evaluate yearly or monthly, openly or behind closed doors, in writing or in dialogue, one-way, two-way or 360 degrees, your staff must clearly understand the criteria for their evaluation.

Introduce your standards of appraisal during the initial hiring process, explain it again during new employee orientation, and clarify the process consistently in staff meetings, newsletters and executive forums.

After you have published these 'rules of the game', keep the playing field fair. Meritocracy demands unprejudiced assessment. Nothing dooms staff morale faster than watching an incompetent who 'takes care of the boss' move up the ladder, while capable staff who don't kiss backsides languish in mediocre positions.

Ask yourself: 'Are the criteria for staff evaluations made clear? Are they openly explained and discussed so that all parties can achieve and succeed? Is the process of evaluation fair-minded?'

If your answers are yes, keep moving forward. If your answers are no or maybe, tackle those issues now. If you are not sure of the answers, check with those whose opinions really count: your staff. Conduct a survey, take a poll, ask for immediate feedback.

But be forewarned: If the staff says your system of appraisal is unclear or less than fair, you'd better be ready to change it. Even more discouraging than an unfair process of evaluation is an unfair process of evaluation that persists after the staff have given you their honest opinions about it.

3. Encourage career development.

Make sure the conversation about career development is always open. Provide high performing staff members with a boss, mentor, counselor or human resouce person who *cares* about their professional growth and personal well-being.

Show you care about your staff members' future possibilities and potential, not just their current results and past achievements. Help the staff understand the competencies required for a more successful future. Chart career progressions that are achievable and realistic.

Provide easy access to courses, seminars and conferences. Subscribe to useful publications and circulate them to your team. Share websites, e-zines and articles of interest. Build a library of books, catalogues, CDs, videos and other career-building resources.

Create opportunities for learning without spending money *outside* your organization by cross-training staff *inside*. Use team rosters and re-assignments to integrate neighboring departments. Create cross-departmental teams to work on cross-functional projects.

Put these career development plans into action and watch your staff's confidence – and competence – grow.

4. Create powerful rewards and meaningful recognition.

Tailor your in-house reward and recognition programs to reinforce the company culture. Most rewards are handed down from the top: management praises staff, supervisor recognizes team member, boss applauds the workers. Why stop there?

Start a 'Bottom-Up' award for staff to recognize their leaders. You set the budget, but allow staff to select the winners, the reasons for winning and the appropriate awards.

Harness positive 'peer pressure' on a group *and* individual basis. Ask each department or team to select and publicly recognize another group for their effort, improvement or support. This encourages cross-functional appreciation, understanding and cooperation.

Ask each staff member to nominate one or two role models from among their peers. Ask for specific reasons supporting each nomination. Then praise the role models *and* publicize the specific reasons to reinforce those values and behaviors.

Invite customers to participate in your staff recognition programs. Put easy-to-use nomination forms at key points of customer contact. Set up a hotline for customers to call with compliments or complaints.

And get your suppliers involved, too. Query them by phone, e-mail or in person. Thank them for their votes and send them a copy of the praise you will share with your staff.

And finally, remember to reward the rewarders! Provide recognition for managers who excel at recognizing the members of their team.

Key Learning Point

It takes energy and commitment to deliver consistently uplifting service. Praise is the spark that lights the fire. Frequent recognition is the fuel that keeps the fire burning. Use plenty of both to keep the climate warm for staff – and the customers they serve.

Action Steps

Conduct a 'recognition audit' inside your organization.

List all the ways your people get appreciated, noticed and rewarded. Sort into categories: individual and group, financial and non-financial, daily, weekly, monthly and yearly, from managers and peers, from customers and suppliers, privately and in public, lavishly and simply, in writing and in person, long running awards and brand new awards, etc.

Which categories are empty or shallow? Get creative with your team and fill them up! (The following pages will help!)

What gets rewarded gets done

Q: What should you highlight with your staff tributes, awards and commendations?

A: What gets rewarded gets done, so recognize and reward a lot!

First, reward all the traditional categories: sales achieved, goals accomplished, customer compliments received. Then add some spice!

Celebrate new accounts, repeat orders, projects completed under budget, money-saving ideas, increased efficiency and, of course, improvements in customer service.

Acknowledge achievements of individuals: most productive person, most consistent performance, most outrageous extra effort!

Applaud improvements made by groups and teams: shortest response time, fastest cycle-time, best collaboration.

Keep your staff motivated with unusual campaigns that arouse interest and lead to productive action.

Highlight the most unusual service recovery or most unique approach to a common problem. Give a 'Most Unexpected Situation' award each month, and put special attention on the learning that followed.

The end of the month is a natural time to give rewards for targets and goals achieved. The end of the quarter aligns with financial accomplishments. The end of the year is an expected time for bonuses, increments and promotions.

But the beginning of each week can also be a good time to set recognition campaigns in motion. And nothing beats the day *before* the weekend for spontaneous cash awards and off-the-wall commendations.

In *The One Minute Manager*, Ken Blanchard and Spencer Johnson encourage readers to 'catch your people doing something right'. That means recognizing good actions whenever and wherever you see them. Give merit to your deserving *'Employee of the Moment'* – why wait for the end of the month or year?

Make your recognition widely known. Give praise in public at staff meetings, management sessions and executive forums. Award prizes at the company picnic or family day. Bestow special honors at the annual kick-off or the end-of-year dinner and dance. Use every opportunity to commend strong performance and recognize spectacular efforts.

Promote awards in the company newsletter. Post them on your website. Notify the local newspaper. Call the radio station for an interview with the winners. Send a photo and caption to your industry publication.

Create a 'Wall of Fame' in your plant, office or building. Take down some of the impersonal decorations and put up visual reminders of your most successful projects and praise-deserving teams.

Make your awards meaningful by giving something the winners will appreciate and remember. If your recipient is outgoing, throw a party, make a fuss, go for all the publicity you can muster.

If the winner is shy, provide your praise in a personal way: a special meeting, a thoughtful letter, a handwritten note on their desk.

When awarding a prize, make the honor reminiscent of the achievement. For the fastest production team, give running shoes. For the engineer who invents a better way, bronze an adjustable wrench and mount it on a plaque. For sales teams that surpass the target, host a darts tournament – bullseye!

Tools and education are practical awards. An extra conference or training session can motivate the technically minded professional. An expensive briefcase can be the symbol of success for a new salesperson just starting out. People have many choices of where to work and how hard to work. An encouraging culture motivates your people to give their best. A sterile or discouraging culture diminishes their enthusiasm daily. Where would *you* rather focus *your* efforts?

One company says, 'If you do a good job, that is your job. Don't expect much recognition.' (That's a culture needing some change!)

Another company says, 'If you do a good job, you will be rewarded, appreciated and praised. Get going!' (Now that's a great place to work.)

Key Learning Point

There are many ways to recognize and reward your staff for achieving high targets of performance. The more praise you give, the more effort and results you will receive.

Action Steps

Work with your team to make a list of all your current targets, goals and objectives. Make the list long with internal and external results desired.

Then ask for a list of all the ways your team would enjoy being appreciated, rewarded and admired. Make the list long with obvious ideas and some outside-the-box suggestions.

Now match the lists in ways that inspire and stimulate everyone's interest. Choose a place to start with a goal to achieve and an interesting reward at the finish. Give it a try. Then try another. And another.

Out-of-this-world recognition and rewards

Brenda at Verifone shares an out-of-this-world recognition approach:

'I found a 23-inch inflatable space alien and we use it for a program called "Above and Beyond". Every time I receive a message that someone has gone above and beyond the call of duty, that person gets to have the alien sit at their desk until the next person gets an "Above and Beyond" compliment or referral.'

Vicki is Director of Customer Service for a successful on-line retailer. She writes:

'We have a monthly award called "Radar O'Reilly". We encourage our associates to share information they have learned: mistakes in our catalog, hard questions from the media, little-known processes that can help everyone, etc. Everyone submits their "Radar" as the events occur and then a winner is selected from the month's submissions. The winner gets a movie ticket!'

Ram is Chief Executive Officer of a large agricultural outfit in India and offers this suggestion:

'The most treasured award in our organization is called the "Bright Spark" Award and is in the form of a Spark Plug mounted on a small rosewood stand. It is given out for the best out-of-the-box idea. It costs hardly anything and yet is the most coveted of awards among our team!'

Key Learning Point

It doesn't take a lot to create an award that *means* a lot!

Action Steps

Create an odd and inexpensive 'award' this month using food, clothing, music, toys or trinkets. Make it fun, make it cheap, make it work!

Bang! You're a winner!

'Right Selection' in Dubai organizes seminars and training programs and distributes great books. They keep their staff motivated with a process costing pennies.

Gautam, General Manager, writes:

At the beginning of the month we distribute six colorful balloons to each staff member in the office. Each time any staff member receives good news – over the phone, fax, or e-mail – he or she blows up a balloon and pops it with a loud bang. Everyone notices and asks what the good news is, which then spreads quickly throughout the office. The first person to burst all six balloons each month wins dinner for two at a restaurant. Then we restart the process with six new balloons each and another free dinner to be won.

This creates a lot of anticipation for good news, followed by excitement and communication each time someone bursts a balloon.

(Good news in our case is qualified and quantified by sales of a minimum amount, a contract confirmed, a client calling to thank us for spectacular service, registration of a large group, confirmation of event sponsors, etc.)

We have been bursting quite a few balloons lately, creating excitement from each person's eagerness to create more frequent positive results. Bang! Another winner!

Key Learning Point

When success is publicized, it can lead to more success. Winning is welcome – and contagious.

Action Steps

Buy a bag of ballons. Pass them out. And start popping!

$50 Jokers and 52 more ways to win

Kym is Managing Director of 'Messages on Hold'. But there's nothing on-hold about the way he encourages service quality and builds loyalty among his staff. Here are three of Kym's simple tips:

1. One way I keep my staff interested in super-serving clients is offering them a 'playing card pick' for every written compliment they receive. They bring me the written compliment and get to pick a playing card from a deck of 53. If they choose a card numbered 2–9 they get the same amount in dollars. Face cards get $10. Aces are worth $20. The joker wins $50! They love this type of simple but fun reward, and it doesn't cost me a fortune!

2. When one of our team excels in service, I write a letter to his or her parents, children or partner saying how great he is and how much we appreciate him in the business. I often receive calls from the recipients saying how grateful they were to read the letter.

3. On the Friday before Father's and Mother's Day, we invite the staff's parents and children to come in for a morning celebration. They are treated like special guests and get a chance to see exactly what their parent or child does with us each business day.

With upbeat ideas like these, no wonder Kym's business, customers and staff are so successful.

Key Learning Point

When one organization employs many ways to praise, the employees tend to stick around – the customers do, too!

Action Steps

Use a range of rewards all at the same time. Use skill and chance. Use family and friends. Use your head, but also use your heart.

Bend the rules to win!

Give a prize each month to the person who bent the rules in the most effective or customer-pleasing manner.

And the prize? Something that bends, of course: exercise bands, a big rubber ball, yoga lessons, a bungee jump, a massage!

Got employees working over-time to complete an important project? Give them a surprise day off from work as thanks.

Is a huge project keeping *everyone* working late? Host a pajama party in the office to let them relax but still be productive. Give prizes for the fanciest or funniest nightwear. Your staff will laugh and learn more about each other – and get energized at the same time.

Ask each employee to write down eight things they would like to receive for reward or recognition – two that cost no money, two that cost $5–$25, two that cost $25–$50 and two that cost $50–$100.

When an employee does something especially terrific for the company or a customer, let them choose one envelope from among the eight, and then give them the item they suggested – and selected.

Key Learning Point

Recognition doesn't need to be formal or financial. Sometimes a softer touch will make a stronger impact.

Action Steps

Look for unusual places and opportunities to reward: in the playground, car wash, hardware and grocery store, drycleaner, beauty parlor, sports stadium, sidewalk, beachfront, ski resort, spa. Everywhere you look are possibilties for positive praise. Make them up, then make them happen!

Sharpen your pencil to build a better service culture

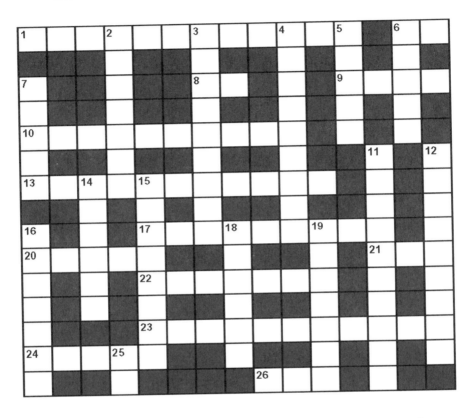

Answers in the Appendix. Which one has got you stumped?

Puzzle clues

Across

1 Contentment at having done something right
6 Two or twice (prefix)
8 An alternative
9 Release steam or express emotion
10 An ____ of goodwill
13 Beyond what is commonly expected
17 Absolutely required
20 Means of communicating information
21 We need to keep problems at ____ or solve them quickly
22 You hope the show was a great ____
23 Advance booking
24 Judge the worth of something
26 Appropriate

Down

2 Exaggerate; enlarge
3 Exceptions to the general rule
4 Significant
5 At no time
6 Incentive; extra
7 Influence or give form to
11 Robust (hyphenated)
12 Pleasure
14 Forthright
15 Happiness
16 Make better
18 Go beyond
19 Without delay; immediate
25 Raise the level (of)

CHAPTER

7

POSITIVE AND POWERFUL PERSPECTIVES

'Seeing the world from a new perpective gives you a
broader view and understanding. Read on!'

Partnership Power: A smart new way to improve your business and your life!

In the beginning, great products were enough to guarantee your business success. With product sophistication, 'six sigma' manufacturing and zero defects you could consistently beat the competition.

But benchmarking, product imitation and reverse engineering came on the scene, and now everyone can make great products.

Then super-fast delivery appeared. Those who produced and shipped products and served their customers quicker were rewarded with growing market share and higher profits. Digital delivery, cycle-time reduction and 24-hour access (by phone and internet) all accelerated commerce – and competition. But now everyone's got a terrific website and courier services cross the planet overnight.

To stay ahead of the competition, excellent-service mindset is coming back into vogue. Being polite, competent and concerned is once again as important as it was in your grandmother's era. And while not every company has mastered this field, competition at the top is intense. Whether you stay at the Sheraton Towers or the Shangri-La, dine at the Rainbow Room or the Hard Rock Café, fly British Airways or Singapore Airlines, the service you receive today will often be quite good.

With competition so intense, winning companies are now growing in still another vital dimension. In addition to great products, rapid delivery and excellent service mindset, market leaders are building stronger *partnerships* with their most valuable clients, suppliers and employees.

What does it mean to build strong partnerships? Why do you need to master this vital skill? What practical steps can you take to achieve it right now?

First, let's put partnership in perspective. There are four different styles of interaction in business (and in life) and three of them are not partnerships at all!

The One-Shot Deal

The first style of interaction is characterized by a short-term focus between the parties. Beyond completing the exchange of the moment, no lasting commitment is intended or implied. Asking someone for directions, buying goods at a close-out sale or picking up a paper from the corner newsstand are all clear examples of the 'one-shot deal'.

Many familiar phrases are associated with this kind of brief and immediate interaction: 'Take it or leave it'; 'What you see is what you get'; 'Here today, gone tomorrow.' With no promise of future involvement between the parties, one more sentence certainly applies: 'Caveat emptor' in Latin. In English: 'Let the buyer beware.'

Transaction Satisfaction

The second style of interaction takes more time than a 'one-shot' deal. More moments of contact are involved in these transactions, and additional effort is required to meet or exceed customer expectations.

Taking a flight from one city to another is an example that includes telephone reservations, airport check-in, on-time departure, drinks, entertainment and service onboard, timely arrival and speedy delivery of checked baggage.

If all of these perception points are well managed, then customers are usually satisfied and a state of affairs called 'transaction satisfaction' exists.

Although no future involvement is promised or required in these transactions, customers often return to vendors and suppliers who consistently meet their transactional needs.

Reliable Relationships

The third style of interaction extends 'transaction satisfaction' into the future. Consistency and dependability are essential, as customers and suppliers count on each other in more frequent business dealings. When done well, this can evolve into a 'reliable relationship' – and both parties benefit over time.

Examples of 'reliable relationships' include daily newspaper delivery, purchases of office supplies on a store credit account, maintenance contracts for essential equipment, and annual checkups with your family doctor.

Powerful Partnerships

The fourth style of interaction also extends into the future, but the value and importance of each interaction grows significantly over time. In a 'powerful partnership' both parties find that working well together brings new possibilities, unique opportunities and otherwise unachievable growth.

A powerful partnership does not grow unattended. Substantial effort and ongoing investments of time, creativity and resources are required to keep a powerful partnership going – and growing.

Examples of powerful partnerships may include research joint ventures, marketing, manufacturing and distribution alliances, excellent manager and secretary combinations and many successful marriages.

Key questions to consider

Which of these four styles of interaction describes your current situation with customers, suppliers, colleagues, managers and employees? Among the four, where are you right now? Where do you want to be?

Four Stages of Improvement

Leaving the 'one-shot' deal aside (it's too short-term for any long-term improvement), let's focus on how to make your transactions more satisfying, your relationships more reliable and your partnerships increasingly powerful.

In each of these styles of interaction, four stages can be identified. Each stage is fertile territory for self-assessment, competitive evaluation and focused action toward improvement. The four stages are *Explore, Agree, Deliver* and *Assure.*

Stage One: Explore

This first stage is the domain of exploration, discovery and open-minded speculation. Both parties must share a commitment to honesty, full disclosure and the desire to create new possibilities together.

Robust exploration can uncover wants, needs, concerns, good and bad past experiences, present constraints, future interests, current priorities and a wide range of competitive and collaborative considerations.

Traditionally this is the domain of marketing, research and strategic visionaries. But the 'explore' quadrant actually plays an essential role in launching most successful interactions, and should be engaged in vigorously by everyone.

This is the time to build rapport, develop an open dialogue and listen carefully for spoken ambitions and unspoken concerns.

Contingency planning begins here with your willingness to discuss the upside and possible downside of the future. Here is where you look together into what can go right – and what might unavoidably go wrong.

How well do *you* explore? Do you regularly meet with your prospects and customers 'just to share ideas'? Or do you contact them only after they call you, or after something has broken down?

Do you survey your market? Do you conduct interviews, customer focus groups and on-site visits? Do you have a method for doing this consistently or is it an *ad hoc* process 'as and when required'?

How easy is it for your customers to *explore* and learn about you? Is your history and philosophy conveniently presented in print and on your website? Can prospects learn quickly about your products, competencies and directions for the future? Do you share stories of how you helped other clients, offering testimonials and references upon request?

If you do not explore well, you may develop the reputation of a mere order taker – responding when required, but only fulfilling direct and straightforward requests.

When you do explore well, you can build a very different public identity: a person who listens well, is interested in the future and who cares about other people's possibilities and concerns. This identity opens up a vast horizon for collaboration, commitment and extended agreements.

Stage Two: Agree

Robust exploration can lead to new opportunities for building the future together. Initial requests and offers become the first steps toward mutually fulfilling agreements.

In business, excellent agreements are clearly documented with a detailed list of specifications and expectations, including quantities, schedules, prices, service levels and warranties (among other things).

In a simple transaction, negotiations toward agreement may be conducted in an atmosphere that is competitive and highly charged. But when you are working toward a relationship or partnership, negotiations should be infused with a different spirit: a shared commitment to win-win agreement and mutual, long-term satisfaction.

Contingency planning is essential at this stage. By carefully thinking through what might go wrong, detailed back-up plans can be agreed to long before they are needed.

Finally, in world-class organizations, the very process of coming to an agreement is itself world-class, with easy-to-understand documentation, user-friendly procedures, around-the-clock access and flexible terms and conditions.

How smoothly and thoroughly do *you* forge your agreements? Do customers marvel at how easy it is to do business with you, or do they complain bitterly about your bureaucratic systems? Do they thank you for your flexibility and understanding, or are they left cold by your rigid 'one-size-fits-all' conditions, products and pricing?

Clear agreements enable effective delivery. Lack of clarity breeds suspicion, uncertainty and misunderstanding. Vague promises may get you started, but if things don't turn out as expected, misunderstanding can lead to disagreement and even escalate to a legal dispute.

In a world that prizes ease of use, saving time and maximum convenience, improving the way you make agreements can give your organization a powerful step up on the competition.

Stage Three: Deliver

With agreements complete, your 'deliver' stage begins.

Here you take all necessary action to fulfill your promises and thoroughly execute your agreements. You serve, develop, customize, manufacture, test, ship, install, modify, upgrade, provide promised training and support.

At this stage you need people who understand what to do and who have the necessary resources to get the job done. This means your delivery team must have a crystal-clear understanding of the promises made in your agreement. It also means they must have the tools, time and training to completely and successfully deliver.

Throughout the delivery stage, it is essential to track progress and keep appropriate parties well informed. If everything goes according to plan, frequent updates can further reinforce confidence among your customers and colleagues. And if the unexpected occurs, the sooner you communicate this to others, the sooner your contingency plans can be launched and put into place.

This willingness and ability to quickly declare 'breakdowns' is an important area where world-class companies differentiate themselves from the rest. While some organizations try to hide bad news and discreetly 'put out the fire', others pride themselves on rapidly alerting all parties so that new actions can be quickly and effectively taken – even capitalizing on unexpected or unintended opportunities.

Stage Four: Assure

In many industries, the ability to deliver on budget and on time has been honed to a fine art with 'six sigma' quality control and cycle-time reduction. But effective delivery does not complete the cycle – not if you are interested in continuing or expanding your involvement over time.

The final stage is 'assure' and is one of the most fertile areas for generating new possibilities in business. In the assure quadrant, you accomplish three vital tasks:

1. Check to see if the promises made on both sides have been fulfilled. If they have, then acknowledge, recognize and reward. If they have not, immediately return to *deliver* and complete the job.

2. Confirm that the needs of your customer have been truly satisfied by the actions you have taken. You may discover that you have faithfully completed all the terms of the agreement, but the original concerns of your customer remain unfulfilled. This is not necessarily the fault of either party and may instead be the result of events that happened in the meantime.

   When this happens, promptly initiate a new round of exploration. Work together to build a more refined set of needs and expectations. Create new agreements to satisfy these needs, and then move forward once again to deliver and assure.

3. Finally, during the assure process, find ways to work even more effectively together the next time. How could the cycle you have just completed be done more quickly or with even better results? What changes should you implement as you move forward into another round of explore, agree, deliver and assure?

Well-planned and sincerely executed assurance can be an effective way of seeking new business. Detailed follow-through often leads to new possibilities, new agreements, new opportunities to deliver.

How well do you and your team members *assure*? Do you consistently follow up with a proven plan of surveys, interviews and on-site customer visits? Or do you subscribe to the old school of 'no news is good news' and wait for disgruntled customers to contact you...if they ever do?

Taking an holistic approach

In many organizations, the four stages of improvement are handled by four different departments: exploration is the realm of marketing; agreements are completed by sales; delivery is the domain of manufacturing, operations and logistics; and assurance is provided, if required, by after-sales warranty and customer service.

Unfortunately, this approach can leave customers with a schizophrenic experience of your organization. Your customers are told one thing by the first department but hear a different story from the next. They cry out for 'one face' to work with rather than an ever-expanding list of business cards, e-mail addresses and telephone numbers.

Inside the organization, this fragmented and specialized approach can lead to mistrust – even outright conflict – between departments.

Fortunately, the solution to this problem can be built right into the procedures and culture of your organization.

First, connect the 'four stages of improvement' with frequent and detailed communication between departments.

Second, institutionalize shared understanding with cross-training, cross-functional teams, and longer-term attachments. The more your people understand what their colleagues are doing, the better your colleagues – and your customers – will be served.

Building a Foundation of Trust

Each time you successfully complete a cycle of explore, agree, deliver and assure, another level of trust is reached between the parties.

This is how humans build trust with one another. We find out what another person is concerned about: we *explore*. We make promises to do something on their behalf: we *agree*. We do what we promised to do: we *deliver*. And then we follow up to be sure they are truly satisfied: we *assure*.

Building trust starts with promises for small items, little issues, minor concerns. After you have proven yourself to be *trustworthy*, then people will open up to share with you and rely on you more.

Want a large order from your customer? Prove yourself with smaller jobs first. Want more responsibility from your boss? Demonstrate your skills and your commitment with a series of well-executed projects.

This makes good sense in business, but it can also apply in your personal and social life. Indeed, building trust with others is the foundation for all successful relationships. Trust is the necessary glue for the partnerships we rely on today – and those we build together for the future.

Service Encounters of the Third Kind

What makes a company successful over the long, long term? What characterizes the service relationship between companies and customers who do business together for decades, even generations?

How can your company stay close to your customers even as times change, technologies change and expectations continually rise?

What can you do to ensure your company's future offers are relevant and valuable in the market?

One powerful step forward is to explore your customers' future needs and interests by cultivating *Service Encounters of The Third Kind*. In these unique encounters, your precious and loyal relationships for the future are built by your words and actions – today.

Let's start by looking closely at Service Encounters of the First and Second Kinds.

Service Encounters Of The First Kind

In Service Encounters of the First Kind, your company approaches the customer with the most basic of all customer service questions: 'What do you want (or need)?'

Your customer replies with equal simplicity, 'I want your product X, by time and date Y, at your listed price Z.'

Your company's priority and service focus should now be clear: Get the customer's order right, and get it right the first time!

Campaigns to accomplish this objective are widespread and easy to spot. 'Do It Right!', 'Zero Defects' and 'Six Sigma Quality' are all examples of slogans companies use to focus their workers on getting the basics right, first time, every time.

In this kind of encounter, breakdowns in service delivery are bad news. They are to be identified, analyzed, solved and, most of all, eliminated. The service system must be streamlined and standardized in every possible way.

Companies that consistently succeed in this undertaking (delivering X by Y at Z price) earn their reputations in the market as steady and reliable suppliers. This leads, as it should, to customer satisfaction.

Training in these organizations is focused on product knowledge, technical skills, thoroughness, accuracy and adhering to proven procedures.

Marketing consists of powerful efforts to push proven products in the market. The customer is 'sold to'.

Looking into the management mindset of these *first kind* organizations, we usually find a keen interest in cutting costs, increasing volume and decreasing cycle-time.

This need for speed is important: Competitors are often closing in with similar products, faster delivery and even lower prices. In this kind of competitive situation, profit margins are paper-thin and companies thrive only through continual increases in volume.

So far so good. But if we look into the staff mindset of such an organization, we find a different way of thinking altogether. Frontline service employees, focused on getting it right the first time, trained to carefully follow all procedures, and encouraged by management to achieve more and more results in less and less time, find themselves answering the phone, opening the mail or meeting the next customer in person thinking to themselves, 'I hope this customer isn't a pain in the neck!'

After all, customers with questions and unusual requests generally take more time, lead to more errors and can result in a general slowing down of the whole system.

No wonder so many customer requests for anything out of the ordinary are met with the retort: 'We don't do it that way' or 'That's not how our procedures work here.'

Service Encounters Of The Second Kind

In Service Encounters of the Second Kind, your company approaches the customer with a question that goes beyond standard offers of X product at Y time and Z price. Instead of the basic 'What do you want?', your service representatives now pose a more inviting question: 'How do you want it?'

Faced with such an open-ended question, the customer naturally replies, 'I want it the way I want it. I want it special. I want it *my way!*'

Your company's service focus must change if you are to deliver what your customer wants just the way your customer wants it. Special products, unique combinations, odd-hour deliveries, different schedules for pricing or payment – all are new challenges for your service team to understand and accomplish.

In Service Encounters of the Second Kind, breakdowns in the service delivery system are to be expected at first – and then overcome. Responsiveness and flexibility become your prime objectives. The organization focuses on being adaptable, accommodating and open to changing requests.

Your service system improves, not through vigorous efforts to standardize but through your willingness and commitment to customize!

Companies that succeed in this challenging undertaking (giving their customers what they want, when and where they want it and just the way they want it) earn their reputations in the market as quick, responsive and open to ongoing change.

When a company is recognized for welcoming and fulfilling unique customer requests, the result is not only customer satisfaction, but a well-deserved and valuable reputation for customer delight.

In these responsive *second kind* organizations, training programs include active listening, creative problem-solving, and attitude-building activities. Staff learn how to find a 'yes' for the customer rather than rolling out the standard 'no'.

Marketing isn't a broadside of mass advertising. Rather, it's a selection of specially modified programs gently pushing customized products to key segments of the market. Customers aren't 'sold to' here, they are served.

In the staff and management mindset of these organizations, we find a shared and sincere commitment to 'bend over backwards' for the customer.

For example, one adapting company proclaims, 'We'll go out of our way for you!' But this catchy phrase reveals the remnants of a first-kind encounter company being forced into second-kind levels of service. Here management is essentially saying: 'We still have *our* way. But don't worry, we'll go *out* of our way just for you.'

You can see this contrast in the advertising of two fast food restaurant chains. A&W features large posters that read: 'You'll love our way!' (That's Service Encounters of the First Kind.)

Compare this with the slogan and jingle for Burger King: 'Have it your way!' (That's Service Encounters of the Second Kind.)

At which establishment will you feel more comfortable saying, 'Two chicken burgers, please. One with extra ketchup and no pickles, and one cooked rare, hold the onions and two packs of mustard on the side.'?

Burger King goes even further with its follow-up campaign: 'Sometimes You've Just Gotta Break the Rules.' That's a direct invitation to highly customized Service Encounters of the Second Kind: 'Have it your way.'

Service Encounters Of The Third Kind

In Service Encounters of the Third Kind, your company welcomes the customer in a manner completely different from the standardized 'What do you want?' or customized 'How do you want it?'.

In a Service Encounter of the Third Kind, your company looks to the customer with interest and patience, and asks the somewhat unlikely question: 'What do you want to become?'

Most customers, if they are given an opportunity to reflect on this very open-ended question, realize that they are, in fact, still a bit uncertain about the future and will reply, 'Actually we're not entirely sure yet.' And then, availing themselves of the sincerity and interest you have shown, might add, 'Could we talk about it together?'

Your question, and their response, opens the door to a very different and collaborative conversation: a Service Encounter of the Third Kind.

Your company's focus shifts again as you enter into a new dialogue with customers, seeking to understand and add value to their plans and possibilities for the future. These conversations, held in a mood of mutual discovery, are concerned with much more than just meeting a customer's existing business requirements. By exploring scenarios and possibilities, you and your customers work together to resolve breakdowns that might emerge only in the future.

For example, innovative financial service companies in Japan consistently ask their customers, 'What do you want to become?' And customers consistently answer, 'I want to become a homeowner, and I want to pass the home on to my children.'

But housing prices in Japan have climbed beyond the average customer's reach. What was the jointly planned and innovative solution? Mortgages with payment terms spanning two generations – and customer relationships that endure beyond a lifetime.

In this *third kind* of customer service, companies must be willing to adapt, modify and in some cases entirely reinvent the purpose and procedures of their business. Rather than 'standardize' or even 'customize' existing products and systems, third-kind companies must make a commitment to 'customer-ize' – to become whatever customers need them to become in order to work together in the future.

For example, railroads in America thought they were in the train business many years ago and nearly went bankrupt asking the customer, 'What type of train car do you want to travel in, where do you want to go to and at what price do you want to travel?' They built coach cars, dining cars, sleeping cars and more.

But since they never asked the customer, 'What do you want to become?', railroad companies did not foresee the need for airborne shipping and travel, and missed evolving into airline companies altogether. Today, government financial support is necessary just to keep American railroads alive.

Companies that do evolve get noticed and earn the respect of customers as relevant, dynamic and constantly changing organizations. They are focused on and committed to the future – not stuck in the success of their past.

Committing to Service Encounters of the Third Kind means you and your customers enter into an intimate and closely linked evolution. As changes in the business environment demand greater innovation, more flexibility and even faster response, you learn to adapt, anticipate and actively support each other.

This association is not based on customer satisfaction or even on customer delight. Instead, the inventive and interactive quality of this relationship is founded on a level of *customer loyalty* that is precious to both parties, and can be vital to a vibrant future.

Competitors can steal away a satisfied customer by offering a little bit more satisfaction, and can even lure away a delighted customer by offering a little more delight. But a *loyal* customer is one who sees his future emerging in part due to your commitment. 'Win-win agreements' and 'building synergy' become passwords for communication between your company and your customer. Adding long-term value is a goal you take responsibility for *together*.

Training programs in third-kind companies highlight the principles of cooperation, collaboration, creativity, invention and design. Real customers and suppliers are featured and included in the real-time training programs.

The customer is no longer sold to, nor simply served. He is genuinely *cared for* through a conscientious relationship that builds trust and momentum over time.

Your service representatives do not 'hard-sell' or 'push' their products. Instead, they work closely with customers to ensure that appropriate products are 'pulled' from your organization. Customers also influence the development of your organization's *future* competencies, capabilities, and commitments.

Staff and management share the same mindset toward the third-kind customer: 'We make your concerns our concerns.' And in such an atmosphere of growing trust, your customer can make similar long-term and loyal commitments back to you. The customer comes to count on you, rely on you and evolve with you.

In the fast-food industry, for example, McDonalds is now test-marketing an all-soy 'veggie burger'. This is in direct response to customers who said, 'We are becoming more health conscious and we want to eat healthier foods.'

Third-kind insurance companies now reap an ever greater slice of the savings and investment pie. Agents no longer ask the simple question, 'Do you want whole life, term or endowment?' Instead leading companies provide their representatives with entirely new categories of investment and insurance products addressing individual concerns and responding to changing needs.

While these are some of the success stories, other companies have missed the importance of third-kind service and teeter dangerously close to the edge of obsolescence.

General Motors, for example, suffered a serious erosion of market share and loyalty before they heard what their customers were saying: 'We want to become more efficient, more cost conscious, and more environmentally friendly.' Other companies listened and delivered appropriately designed new cars. Customers responded, giving back profits and gains in market share.

Intricate slide rules were famous for aiding calculation in my father's day. Manufacturers diligently asked the engineers, 'How do you want it?' and built an impressive range of slide rules in response: wooden, plastic, steel, large, pocket-sized, flat, round and double-sided.

But they never asked what customers were 'becoming', so didn't hear their customers' growing urge for things instantaneous and electronic. The firms that built a wide range of precision slide rules are now gone. Not one slide rule maker is among the calculator and computer manufacturers of today.

From carbon paper to photocopies, buggy whips to stick shifts, typewriters to computers, copper wire to fiber optics, smoke signals to wireless, each evolution begs the question, 'What happened to those companies?' Did they make the switch? Did they survive? Did they move from 'What do you want?' to 'What do you want to become?'

In an environment of continually accelerating change, the only certainty we have is that the future will be different from today. The opportunities for evolution and collaboration with your customers will be endless.

What about your company? Will you gradually go out of business with a standardized service system that provides efficient answers to questions your customers no longer ask?

Or will you change the tone and tenor of your service encounters from the order taker asking, 'What do you want?' and the order maker's, 'How do you want it?' to the loyal business partner who patiently and intelligently asks, 'What do you want to become?'

This change requires a new mindset and new methods for engaging with your customers and suppliers. It's called Service Encounters of the Third Kind. Learn it.

Medical Encounters of the Third Kind

Dear Mr. Kaufman,

I'm a practicing medical doctor.

I came across your video playing at the bookstore. I was rooted to the spot for 30 minutes! I bought your book and subscribed to your newsletter. Thoroughly enjoyed them both!

Regarding your Service Encounters of the Third Kind, how do I apply that in my medical practice? The first and second kind are no problem. But how can I use the *third kind* in medicine? How do I ask, 'What do you want to become?' to my patients?

Dr. H.H., Kuala Lumpur, Malaysia

*   *   *

Hello, Dr H.H.,

Thank you for that great question!

Service Encounters of the Third Kind in medicine moves the doctor/patient relationship beyond 'What's wrong or what needs fixing?' (an encounter of the first kind), beyond 'Which therapy or style of treatment do you want?' (an encounter of the second kind), to a dialogue focusing on your patient's preferred choice of lifestyle: nutrition, exercise, bodywork, stress release and emotional well-being included.

This is a proactive conversation about changing behaviors and practices to *create* and *achieve* intended health objectives. It's not a traditional (often remedial) conversation about what's wrong and what needs to be, or can be, fixed.

 In medicine these third-kind discussions are usually seen as preventative in nature, and often aren't easy to broach given the intense pressures of time most doctors face, and given the traditional view most patients have of their doctors.

However, some chiropractors, naturopaths and holistic medical practitioners have built successful practices in the third-kind direction. They provide education for their patients on movement (yoga, exercise, breath work), nutrition (supplements, dietary choices, cooking styles), and even family and career matters (stress clinics, relationship workshops, company wellness retreats).

I am not sure where your practice is along this spectrum, but I do hope this reply is useful for you. Wishing you and your patients the very best.

Ron Kaufman

Key Learning Point

Many professionals are moving from first-kind encounters to second-kind interactions to truly third-kind conversations and commitments with their customers. Those who engage customers in such proactive conversations will invent a successful future more assuredly than those who only satisfy immediate customer demands.

Action Steps

Gather a group of colleagues and customers to explore the question, 'What do you want to become?' Imagine and create new possibilities for customers, for colleagues, for your company. Don't get caught with all your attention on the requirements of today. The future of your business is already forming in the possibilities you can imagine for tomorrow.

In challenging times, service matters most!

As the wind of economic cycles blows hard, some businesses try to contain costs by cutting corners on customer service. This is exactly the *wrong* thing to do, because service matters now more than ever. Here's why:

A. When people buy during an economic downturn they are extremely conscious of the hard-earned money that they spend. Customers want *more attention*, more appreciation and more recognition when making their purchases with you, not less.

B. Customers want to be sure they get maximum value for the money they spend. They want assistance, education, training, installation, modifications and support. The basic product may remain the same, but they want *more service*.

C. Customers want firmer guarantees that their purchase was the right thing to do. In good times, a single bad purchase can be quickly overlooked or forgotten, but in tough times, every expenditure is scrutinized. *Provide the assurance* your customers seek with generous service guarantees, regular follow-up and speedy follow-through on all queries and complaints.

D. In difficult economic times, people spend less time traveling and 'wining and dining', and more time carefully shopping for each and every purchase. *Giving great service* enhances the customer's shopping experience and boosts your own company's image.

When times are good, people move fast and sometimes don't notice your efforts. In tougher times, people move more cautiously and *notice every extra effort* you make.

E. When money is tight, many people experience a sense of lower self-esteem. *When they get good service* from your business, it boosts their self-image. And when they feel good about themselves, they feel good about you. And when they feel good about you, they buy.

F. In tough times, people talk more with each other about saving money and getting good value. *Positive word-of-mouth* is a powerful force at any time. In difficult times, even more ears will be listening. Be sure the words spoken about your business are good ones!

The Secrets of Superior Service

Giving good service in tough times makes good business sense. But how do you actually achieve it? Here are eight proven principles you can use. I call them *The Secrets of Superior Service*.

1. Understand how your customers' expectations are rising and changing over time. What was good enough last year may not be good enough now. Use customer surveys, interviews and focus groups to understand what your customers really want, what they value and what they believe they are getting (or not getting) from your business.

2. Use quality service to differentiate your business from your competition. Your products may be reliable and up-to-date – but your competitors' goods are, too. Your delivery systems may be fast and user-friendly, but so are your competitors'!

   You can make a more lasting difference by providing personalized, responsive and extra-mile service that stands out in a unique way your customers will appreciate – and remember.

3. Set and achieve high service standards. You can go beyond basic and expected levels of service to provide your customers with desired and even surprising service interactions. Determine the standard for service in your industry, and then find a way to go beyond it. Give

more choice than 'the usual', be more flexible than 'normal', be faster than 'the average', and extend a better warranty than all the others.

Your customers will notice your higher standards. But eventually those standards will be copied by your competitors, too. So don't slow down. Keep stepping up!

4. Learn to manage your customers' expectations. You can't always give customers everything their hearts desire. Sometimes you need to bring their expectations into line with what you know you can deliver.

The best way to do this is by first building a reputation for making and keeping clear promises. Once you have established a base of trust and good reputation, you only need to ask your customers for their patience in the rare instances when you cannot meet their first requests. Nine times out of ten they will extend the understanding and the leeway that you need.

The second way to manage customers' expectations is to 'under promise, then over deliver'. Here's an example: you know your customer wants something done *fast*. You know it will take an hour to complete. Don't tell your customer it will take an hour. Instead, let them know you will *rush* on their behalf, but promise a 90-minute timeframe.

Then, when you finish in just one hour (as you knew you would all along), your customer will be delighted to find that you finished the job 'so quickly'. That's 'under promise, then over deliver'.

5. Bounce back with effective service recovery. Sometimes things *do* go wrong. When it happens to your customers, do everything you can to set things right. Fix the problem and show sincere concern for any discomfort, frustration or inconvenience. Then *do a little bit more* by giving your customer something positive to remember – a token of goodwill, a gift of appreciation, a discount on future orders, an upgrade to a higher class of product.

This is not the time to assign blame for what went wrong or to calculate the costs of repair. Restoring customer goodwill is worth the price in positive word-of-mouth and new business.

6. Appreciate your complaining customers. Customers with complaints can be your best allies in building and improving your business. They point out where your system is faulty or your procedures are weak and problematic. They show where your products or services are below expectations. They point out areas where your competitors are getting ahead or where your staff is falling behind. These are the same insights and conclusions companies pay consultants to provide. But a complainer gives them to you free!

   And remember, for every person who complains, there are many more who don't bother to tell you. The others just take their business elsewhere...and speak badly about you. At least the complainer gives you a chance to reply and set things right.

7. Take personal responsibility. In many organizations, people are quick to blame others for problems or difficulties at work: managers blame staff, staff blame managers, Engineering blames Sales, Sales blames Marketing and everyone blames Finance. This does not help. In fact, all the finger-pointing make things much worse.

   Blaming yourself doesn't work, either. No matter how many mistakes you may have made, tomorrow is another chance to do better. You need high self-esteem to give good service. Feeling ashamed doesn't help.

   It doesn't make sense to make excuses and blame the computers, the system or the budget, either. This kind of justification only prolongs the pain before the necessary changes can take place.

   The most reliable way to bring about constructive change in your organization is to take personal responsibility and help make good things happen. When you see something that needs to be done, do it. If you see something that needs to be done in another department, recommend it. Be the person who makes suggestions, proposes new ideas and volunteers to help on problem solving teams, projects and solutions.

8. See the world from each customer's point of view. We often get so caught up in our own world that we lose sight of what our customers actually experience.

Make time to stand on the other side of the counter or listen on the other end of the phone. Be a 'mystery shopper' at your own place of business. Or become a customer of your best competition. What you notice when you look from the 'other side' is what your customers experience every day.

Finally, always remember that *service* is the currency that keeps our economy moving. I serve you in one business, you serve me in another. When either of us improves, the economy gets a little better. When both of us improve, people are sure to take notice. When everyone improves, the whole world grows stronger and closer together.

The time to make it happen is now.

How does Singapore Airlines fly so high?

As a professional speaker, I often share stories and examples of companies that deliver great service. One company that's easy to talk about is Singapore Airlines.

Profitable every year since the beginning, Singapore Airlines (SIA) frequently wins international awards for top service and in-flight quality. Here's how they do it:

1. **Clarity and Commitment.**

   SIA's focus on service is absolutely clear. The mission statement and core values establish, without question, that quality service to customers is a fundamental objective and aspiration of the airline. Every major issue, question or decision is considered in light of their commitment to providing world-class customer service.

2. **Continuous Training.**

   Training is not a one-time affair. SIA understands that daily customer contact can be draining and that customer expectations are always on the rise.

   To meet this challenge, four training divisions within the company (Cabin Crew, Flight Operations, Commercial and Management Development) offer a wide range of inspiring and demanding educational programs. Whether in the classroom, through full-scale simulations or on the job, SIA staff members are continually motivated to upgrade, uplift and improve their performance.

Training is not conducted just during robust economic times. Even during the downturns, SIA's investment in training goes on. This gives the airline a twofold advantage. First, it allows SIA to surge ahead in quality service when other carriers cut back. Second, it demonstrates to all SIA staff that continuous learning and improvement are essential principles for success, not just nice-to-have bonuses.

3. **Career Development.**

SIA staff are regularly appraised for performance *and* potential. High-flyers (high performance *and* potential) are identified early and given every opportunity to learn and grow. Senior managers are effectively developed with frequent rotation through top positions in the company. This leads to a management team with great breadth and depth, with a shared understanding of 'the big picture', and with a commitment to do what's best for the customers and the business, not just for one department or another.

4. **Internal Communication.**

SIA is a large organization, with more than 28,000 staff (including subsidiaries) located around the world. People from different cultures work together to produce a seamless and consistently positive customer experience. In the pilot pool alone more than 25 countries are represented!

To keep everyone on the same wavelength, SIA publishes a variety of department newsletters, websites and a monthly company-wide magazine.

Regular dialogue sessions between management and staff keep communication flowing. A program called 'Staff Ideas in Action' ensures that new suggestions for improvement are constantly put forward. Semi-annual business meetings provide another forum for sharing and evaluating results in sales, marketing, yields and customer satisfaction levels.

5. **Consistent External Communication.**

Whether their advertisement is about new destinations, new airplanes, onboard cuisine, or new seats and entertainment services, the legendary 'SIA Girl' is always featured.

Why? Because the bottom line for SIA is not the plane, seat, entertainment or destination. The bottom line is delivering high-quality service, and the 'SIA Girl' *is* the brand identity, the personification of that service.

Of course everyone knows it takes the entire SIA team to deliver excellent service, but showing a picture of a smiling engineer, a competent pilot or a friendly telephone reservations agent would not carry the same consistency in external communication: The 'SIA Girl' represents impeccable quality service. In the airline's external communication, she is always there.

6. **Connection with Customers.**

SIA makes a concerted effort to stay in touch with customers through in-flight surveys, customer focus groups and rapid replies to every compliment or complaint they receive. SIA then consolidates this input with other key data to create a quarterly 'Service Performance Index' that is *very* closely watched throughout the airline.

Frequent flyers are kept well-connected with special messages, attractive offers and publications sent regularly to Priority Passenger Service (PPS) members. And *very* frequent flyers achieve an elite 'Solitaire' status with a wide range of valuable privileges: most convenient check-in, additional baggage allowance, priority seating and waitlisting, and more. (I am one of those very frequent flyers, and I enjoy it!)

7. Benchmarking.

The airline industry is intensely competitive with every carrier seeking new ways to 'get ahead of the pack'. SIA tracks competitors' progress closely. Even outside the airline industry, SIA looks for new ways to improve and grow. When hotels, banks, restaurants, retail outlets and other service industries take a step forward in their amenities, convenience or comfort, SIA watches closely to see what can be adopted or adapted for the airline industry.

8. Improvement, Investment and Innovation.

From the earliest days, SIA has built a solid reputation for taking the lead and doing things differently, introducing free drinks and headsets, fax machines onboard, individual video screens and telephones in every seat, cutting-edge gaming and in-flight entertainment, 'book the cook' service for special meals in First and Business Class, telephone, fax, e-mail and internet check-in, innovative cargo facilities – the list goes on and on.

This commitment to continuous improvement is coupled with a cultural determination to try it out, make it work and see it through. Not every innovation succeeds and some are eventually removed from service (the fax machines are long gone), but SIA makes every possible effort to find the key to success – or to create it.

9. Rewards and Recognition.

While excellent staff performance is rewarded with increased pay and positions, the most prestigious award is reserved for truly superior service.

The 'CEO's Transforming Customer Service Award' is given annually to teams and individuals who respond to unique customer situations with exceptionally positive, innovative or selfless acts of service. This award carries no financial benefit, but it is the most revered accolade in the airline. Winners and their families are flown to Singapore for a special dinner celebration, the

POSITIVE AND POWERFUL PERSPECTIVES | **213**

story of their efforts is published in the monthly magazine, and their personal status as a 'Managing Director's Award Winner' remains a badge of distinction for life.

10. Professionalism, Pride and Profits.

The result of these efforts is a staff culture vigorously committed to customers and continuous improvement.

Staff pride and sense of ownership are evident in the way they protect the airline's reputation and participate in programs like the 'aircraft adoption' scheme.

Good profits are also achieved, but not as an end in themselves. Rather, SIA's profits are 'the applause we receive for providing consistent quality and service to our customers'.

Does all this mean that SIA is perfect? Of course not. Even SIA cannot satisfy every customer every time. Bags go astray, telephone lines become congested, and meals at 39,000 feet are not always perfectly deluxe. There will always be room for improvement.

With a track record of success, SIA must work doubly hard to avoid becoming complacent. Managers must be open to change and not become arrogant or defensive. Staff must be proud of the airline yet remain eager for passenger suggestions, recommendations and constructive criticism.

The definition of a truly loyal airline customer is someone who is pleased with the service, flies with the airline again, recommends the airline to others and takes the time and effort to point out ways the airline can still improve.

I look forward to my flights on SIA and I use the carrier two or three times each month. My speeches and training programs are peppered with positive stories from the airline's history and lore. And my mail to SIA includes plenty of ideas and suggestions to help them improve.

Singapore Airlines has earned my loyalty on the ground and in the sky. They've got a great way to fly – and to run a highly successful business.

Figure it out: Which point of view is right for you?

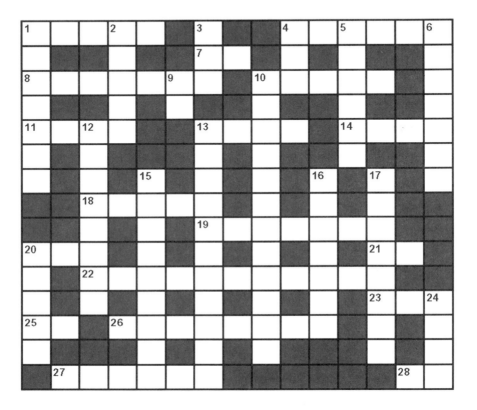

If you need them, find the answers are in the Appendix.

But all the clues are on page 215, and the answers are waiting in your mind.

Puzzle clues

Across

1	Express feeling
4	The courage to carry on
7	Raise
8	Progress
10	Swiftness
11	Strive; make an effort
13	Engage for service
14	Try something
18	Construct
19	Accept hospitably
20	Suffer from sickness
21	Proceed
22	A sudden brilliant idea
23	An overwhelming feeling of admiration
25	Either/____
26	Associates with common benefits
27	Up-to-date
28	Exist

Down

1	Set a good ____
2	Impart skills or knowledge
3	That which is deserved or owed
4	Delineate or arrange
5	The popular tastes at a given time
6	Rapid transport of goods
9	Together or joint (prefix)
10	Hair-triggered (2 words)
12	Denoted by signs and/or marks
13	The most meaningful personal notes are ____
15	Method of joint property ownership
16	Net gains after expenses
17	A ____ pause
20	Improvised; impromptu
24	Customers should feel at ____ and comfortable

CHAPTER

8

TOOLS AND TIPS FOR TERRIFIC TRAINING

Anything is easier when you've got the right tools for the job. This chapter gives you the right tools. Use them!

Ten ways to maximize the impact of training

Training your staff is an essential investment in today's changing and competitive environment. But just sending staff to attend training programs is not enough. You should maximize the impact of your investment by following these key guidelines before, during and after the training.

Before the training program:

1. Review with staff why they were selected for the program and discuss anticipated benefits for the organization. This shifts their perspective from purely personal, 'I am going to attend a training', to personal and organizational, 'The organization is making an investment so I can attend a training. The purpose of this investment is to help me upgrade my skills so that my team and our organization becomes more effective.'

2. Ask participants to talk about how they might benefit from the program. Where do they see opportunities for improvement in their own skills and/or behavior?

3. Discuss and obtain agreement from your staff for their punctuality, attendance and active participation in the training program.

4. Redistribute participants' workloads so they don't return to a mountain of pending matters. This helps participants keep their minds focused on the course.

5. If sending more than one participant, create a 'buddy system' before they go. Buddies should work together to ensure each participates fully and gains maximum value from the training.

During the training program:

6. If the course is more than one day, have participants brief their managers as the course progresses. This can be done in a short face-to-face meeting, a telephone call at the end of the day, or in a summary by e-mail.

   Participants should identify what material was covered during the day, what new learning occurred and what value they see in applying this learning back at work.

7. Discuss any ambiguities or uncertainties from the course material that may arise. Help participants identify key learning points and examples of their application on the job. If needed, help write clarifying questions for participants to take back to the course instructor on the following day.

8. If there are interim assignments to complete, engage others who are not attending the course in discussions and deliberations. This brings the learning experience back into the office, building an internal support network during and after the training.

After the training program:

9. Meet with participants to review:

   What were the most valuable lessons from this program?

   What will you now do differently? In which situations?

   When will you begin or try this new approach?

   What suggestions do you have to improve or customize the course?

   Who else do you believe should attend this particular training program?

10. Discuss organizational improvements that could be implemented based on the participants' new learning. Be willing to try new suggestions on a trial basis with the course participants closely involved in implementing and tracking results.

Ten keys to a successful management retreat

Management retreats are tremendous opportunities to review, assess, align and move your team forward. Get the most out of your next retreat through effective planning and preparation.

These ten keys can help you unlock the amazing power of your meeting:

1. Select your site with care.

Your management retreat can be held on-site (at your place of work), or off-site (at a home, hotel or conference venue). Each has its advantages:

On-site events keep costs low and familiar business facilities close at hand.

Off-site events reduce distraction and can promote a 'big picture' perspective.

Be careful not to mismatch your event theme and conference facility. If your theme is 'nose to the grindstone', don't hold your retreat at Disneyland. If your theme is 'stepping back to view the horizon', don't hold your retreat in a busy downtown conference center.

2. Design your sequence with care.

The timing of your entire agenda is key to your success. Decide early whether you want a high-intensity working event, a laid-back and relaxing retreat or a balanced program combining both styles.

If you intend to combine work and play, carefully consider which should be first.

'Work first, play later' gives participants something to look forward to, and a reason to get through business issues quickly.

'Play first, work later' sets a tone of enjoyment for the program and puts work issues closer to your return to the office.

'Work, play, work' lets you get started on business issues, take a break and then come back to complete your work after gaining some recreational perspective.

3. **Circulate a pre-retreat agenda.**

   Let people know what your objectives are for the retreat and the sequence of the program they will attend.

   Give everyone an opportunity to prepare for full and constructive participation. If they need to bring information, give a presentation, participate in a panel or work on a team, let them know well in advance.

4. **Use breaks to your advantage.**

   Use meals and coffee-breaks to make progress in your program. Arrange seating at meals to foster communication. Turn some coffee breaks into 'working breaks' with refreshments inside the conference room.

   Select food very carefully. Avoid fried foods and heavy gravies – both put participants to sleep!

   Start lunches with salad, not soup. Salad can be served in an instant or be on the table when your participants arrive. Soup takes time to come hot from the kitchen, gets cold quickly and can set your entire agenda back by 10–20 minutes if it is not ready on time.

   If you plan to serve alcohol during dinner, let the evening events be pure fun. Alchohol and focused attention don't mix well together.

5. Present new perspectives.

Create a perspective not usually seen at the office. Bring in examples from outside your industry to highlight key points. Engage external speakers to share cross-industry knowledge and unique expertise.

6. Involve customers as your guests.

Bring in customers for specific portions of your retreat. Golf games are traditional, but customer panels and discussion groups can also yield valuable results.

7. Involve suppliers as your guests.

Strengthening your partnership with suppliers makes good business sense. Suppliers can add unique value to your management retreat by sharing their perspective and competitive industry awareness.

8. Circulate post-retreat actions and agreements.

Put decisions and new action plans in writing. Send copies to retreat participants with an encouraging or congratulatory note from the top.

9. Gather input and recommendations.

After the event, or before everyone departs, gather their ideas for further improvement. Ask what participants want more of, and less of, at your next retreat.

10. Use an outside process facilitator.

It can be useful to engage a professional facilitator to help with your retreat. Outside talent can bring years of experience to help design your event. A competent external facilitator can also serve as a 'neutral party', making sure that everyone speaks and is heard.

If you do engage an outside facilitator, don't let him or her get caught uninformed! Be sure to provide detailed information about your business – and about the personalities attending your event.

Ten ways to leverage a professional speaker

Hiring a professional speaker can be an effective way to raise an issue, educate an audience or drive home a business message. Use these top ten ideas to get the most value from your investment.

1. **Use pre-event publicity to build interest in your speaker.**

   Use posters to announce the speaker and the topic.

   Send a memo describing the speaker's credentials.

   Encourage your staff to visit the speaker's website.

2. **Fully inform your speaker about your business.**

   Provide information for the speaker to study well in advance: annual reports, newsletters, press releases, etc.

   Answer the speaker's questionnaire as completely as possible. Don't hold back useful insights or information.

3. **Put your speaker in touch with people in the business.**

   Give your speaker access with management and staff prior to the event. Telephone conversations are a good start. Face-to-face meetings are even better.

4. **Put your speaker in touch with your customers.**

   Encourage contact between your speaker and your customers. Let customers know in advance that a speaker will be calling to gather their ideas and suggestions.

5. **Be candid with your speaker about your culture and your competition.**

   Let your speaker know what's really going on in your industry. Be sure he or she understands your competitive advantage and the actions being taken by others.

6. **Review and use a speaker's introduction.**

Your speaker should provide you with a 'speaker's introduction' in advance of the actual event. Customize this to link with your event theme or business issues.

The person introducing the speaker should be prepared and enthusiastic. The introduction starts the speech!

7. **Reinforce the message with take-home handouts.**

Help people remember and apply key points with an attractive take-home handout. Handouts can be as extensive as a a customized notebook, or as simple as a laminated wallet-size card.

8. **Arrange for audio and video taping of your speaker.**

If your speaker is properly prepared and effective in delivering an important message, the cost of professional audio and video taping can be a very wise investment.

9. **Improve room setup with your speaker's input.**

Be sure your speaker has access to the venue prior to his or her presentation. Professional speakers have vast experience with room layouts, acoustics, lighting, etc. Small improvements can make a very big difference.

10. **Allow time for questions and answers, but ensure you get good questions!**

When the schedule allows, a Q&A session lets your audience go deeper into the topic with the speaker.

Get good questions by letting your audience know in advance that a Q&A session will follow the normal presentation. Allow a few minutes for discussion among audience members before taking the first question. Make sure one or two participants are ready in advance with excellent questions to help 'get the ball rolling'.

Provide microphones for your audience to ask questions. Otherwise, ask your speaker to repeat each question clearly before providing an answer.

How to use 'Ron Kaufman's Active Learning Toolbox'

Why are some training programs so dull, and others so full of active participation? What makes one trainer plod along, while another is well-known for bringing energy and effectiveness to each session?

Over the years I have developed a technique that generates active participation every time, even with the most reserved students and in the most conservative cultures. I use it for workshops, team building programs, course curriculum and conferences. I use it once or twice for quick icebreakers, and over and over again for longer-term educational programs.

I call it 'Ron Kaufman's Active Learning Toolbox'. The box has four key components, each of which is essential to your success. Here's how the components work together.

1. Who am I doing this with?

People must be very clear about who they are working with. Is this an exercise to be done alone? Am I supposed to work with a partner? Is this a task for everyone in the room to work on together? Should we tackle this with the folks seated around our table?

Who should I be working with right now?

2. How much time do we have?

Is this a task to be done in the next ten minutes or should we prepare our answers overnight? Is there a need for speed ('Complete this as quickly as possible.') or is the time clearly fixed ('You will have until 11:00 am to finish.')?

How much *time* do we have to get this done?

3. What content are we focusing on?

Are we sharing our opinions on a topic? Or comparing our experiences in the field? Are we working on a case-study, discussing a video, debating a presentation or refuting an article we've been asked to read?

What *content* do you want us to focus on during the time we have to work together?

4. What output are we supposed to create?

Do you want us to come up with one answer for the group? Or a list of five possibilities to discuss? Do you want us to prioritize problems to be resolved? Or generate a series of action steps with dates, responsibilities and outcomes?

What *output* do you expect us to create or complete in the time we have to work on this content together?

When all four elements (who, time, content and output) are clearly understood, people *will* participate. If any of these areas are unclear or uncertain, many will hesitate.

Here are some examples of putting 'Ron Kaufman's Active Learning Toolbox' to work. Notice how each example clearly explains *who, time, content* and *output*.

New group introductions:

Sit in groups of four with people you do not know well. Take two minutes each to describe the nature of your work, who you serve and who serves you. Listen carefully to what others in your group say about themselves. After each person has spoken, take the next four minutes to discuss what you have in common at work and what is different.

Who: groups of four. Time: twelve minutes total. It may help to ring a bell at appropriate intervals to keep the groups on time. Content: participants' actual work and their daily service contacts. Output: relevant sharing of information and resulting familiarization among those in the group.

Learning with an in-class or on-line video:

Select one person to be your partner. Watch this ten-minute video together. Discuss for four minutes what you and your partner consider to be the top learning points in the video, and which you agree is the most important for your work. The partner with longer hair (or darker shoes) will present your choice of 'most important point' to the whole group.

Who: you and a partner. Time: fourteen minutes total for video and discussion. Content: a pre-selected video. Output: one partner prepared to present a key learning point.

In the next set of examples, notice how the *output* of each exercise becomes *content* for the exercise that follows. Using this simple technique, your meeting or workshop will enjoy a natural flow of participation and cascading value.

Find the Service Problems:

Sit with your department and choose a scribe to write at the flipchart. In five minutes, brainstorm all current service problems in your department. The department with the longest list 'wins'.

Who: all department members, one scribe. Time: five minutes. Content: current service problems. Output: longest possible list.

Focus on the issues:

As a department, review the prior list for ten minutes. Consolidate the service problems into four or five key issues. Make a new list with only those key issues on the chart.

Who: all department members, one scribe. Time: ten minutes. Content: previously generated list of service problems. Output: consolidated service issues.

Prioritize for improvement:

Each person gets five stickers, numbered 1 to 5. Everyone votes to prioritize issues from the prior list by placing their stickers on the flipchart: 5 = top priority, 1 = lowest. Tally the votes. Then rewrite the list so the issue with highest number of votes is on top, lowest on the bottom.

Who: all group members. Time: immediately. Content: the previous list of consolidated service issues. Output: group prioritization of the issues.

Can you imagine the next applications of 'Ron's toolbox' ?

Divide into groups based on the top three issues. Each group brainstorms a list of solutions then prioritizes the list. One group member presents the prioritized solutions. Others in the department raise two appropriate questions. This process delivers layer after layer of value and is bound only by your need for results – and your imagination.

This active learning technique works best when people understand 'what's in it for them'. Here's how you can use the 'toolbox' to focus on this vital issue from the beginning:

In groups, take four minutes and make a list of all the benefits to be gained by learning more about this topic. The person in your group with the shortest hair (or most colorful shirt, or largest watch, or shortest tenure in the organization) will be asked to share one idea from your list. It must be a different idea than those already shared by others. Be sure your list is long enough so your group representative will still have something to say!

Can you see how this couples two applications of the 'toolbox' into an effective first exercise? With some experience and experimentation, you will find 'toolbox' sequences that work well for you, your participants and your topics.

I use 'Ron Kaufman's Active Learning Toolbox' to create successful workshops, conferences and other learning programs. Everyone enjoys and *participates* in these events.

How do I make that happen? By constantly changing the answer to these four essential questions: *Who* am I working with? How much *time* do we have? What *content* are we focusing on? What *output* do you want from us?

Now you can do it, too.

Ten great reasons to use a training game at your next conference

A well-designed, well-delivered training game can get your audience involved with your topic – and with each other.

Here are ten great reasons to use a training game at your next conference or special event.

1. Break and melt the ice.

Games give everyone the opportunity to break out of traditional roles and express themselves more freely. New staff can step up to lead. Senior managers can let go and let loose. A great way to begin!

2. Draw out quiet or new participants.

Games can require everyone to contribute in order for anyone to achieve success. New or quiet participants will have to participate 'more than usual' and can quickly become valued members of the group.

3. Reveal hidden issues.

What isn't seen, discussed or understood in 'real life' can come screaming to the surface through a well-designed training actvity or game. Expert processing can then help participants recognize the real issues at stake and openly discuss the implications.

4. Reveal hidden talents.

Who knows what skills and talents lie just below the surface of your colleagues? The right game roles, rules and conditions can set everyone loose to invent, create, design, negotiate, set new targets, take bold actions and succeed.

5. **Generate a mood of energy and enjoyment.**

   Conference games let people have fun. A good game will deliver key learning points with involvement, energy, excitement and entertainment. What a great way to launch your program or wrap up the entire event!

6. **Establish a reference point or introduce a metaphor.**

   People refer to effective training games and activities for many years. Insights from your conference game can become a positive anchor for long-term understanding and cooperation.

7. **Highlight a specific theme.**

   Whether your focus is teamwork, leadership, customer service, competition, motivation or innovation, an effectively designed game can bring that theme to 'front of mind' – and keep it there throughout your event.

8. **Gather new ideas.**

   Games put participants in a totally different context. All kinds of new ideas and insights tend to appear. The best ideas can be captured at the conference and pursued long after it is over.

9. **Game solutions can become work solutions.**

   What succeeds in a game may succeed in the real world, too. Lessons learned in conference games can be useful throughout the year. Be sure to note the link between work and games when all the fun is over.

10. **Games add energy to the mix.**

   Every conference should include a healthy mix of methods and techniques: speeches, workshops, exhibitions, demonstrations, meals and breaks, social gatherings, interactive presentations. And, in the right situations, effective, entertaining and energizing training games.

Ten innovative ideas for successful team building events

Team building can give a powerful boost to the spirit and effectiveness of any group. Well-designed and delivered team building programs can lead your group to a better understanding, clearer alignment and much stronger motivation to work and succeed together.

Organizing a team building event is a big responsibility. The next time the responsibility lands on your shoulders, use these ten ideas to make your event a well-planned and memorable success.

1. Set the tone with an inspiring theme.

Telegraph the tone and purpose of your event with a theme that hits the mark. 'The Third Annual Team Building Program' is not going to excite many participants.

Here are examples of themes my clients have used to motivate and communicate with their teams: 'Rocket to the Top, Together!' (for a software company seeking to achieve dominant market share), 'The Winning Team' (for a financial services group seeking to overcome competitors and economic adversity), 'Forging a New Alliance' (for a diverse medical services group managing a complete reorganization of roles and departments).

2. Prime the pump for full participation.

Use internal communication to get everyone interested and ready for the event. Use e-mail, printed memos, websites, bulletin boards, posters and meetings to arouse people's curiosity, and circulate a list of objectives and issues for the meeting.

You could conduct a survey prior to the meeting and announce the results during the program. Have individuals prepare essential business presentations. Create cross-functional teams to deliver the evening entertainment.

3. **Conduct the program off-site.**

Major team-building programs are frequently conducted off-site. This allows participants to get away from the workplace physically (minimizing disruptions) and mentally (opening their thinking to new points of view).

4. **Use a mix of energy, enterprise and entertainment.**

Stimulate interest and involvement by employing a full range of team building activities. You can have 'work hard' sections with speeches about the future and workshops on current business problems. You can have 'play hard' sections with team games or outdoor challenges. And you can include social sections with mealtime activities, awards and evening entertainment.

Carefully sequence your activities throughout the day and evening. Be especially careful to follow lunches with some physical activity and to end your program with a strong note of confidence and commitment.

5. **Allow enough time to process, discuss and apply.**

Allow some time between each activity for discussion about new learning and application to the job. It's better to have a full day with two team building games and enough time for discussion, than a 'stuffed' day with three or four games but little time for reflection.

6. **Focus on new actions with 'more, less, start, and stop'.**

During the program, have participants develop clear answers to the following questions:

'What do you want (the other person, department, etc.) to do *more* of?'

'What do you want (the other person, department, etc.) to do *less* of?'

'What do you want (the other person, department, etc.) to *start* doing?'

'What do you want (the other person, department, etc.) to *stop* doing?'

Toward the end of your program, have participants make a list of personal commitments:

'What am I committed to do *more* of?'

'What am I committed to do *less* of?'

'What am I committed to *start* doing?'

'What am I committed to *stop* doing?'

7. **Use photos and videos to extend the program's impact.**

Engage a photographer to document your team building program. Give copies of special photographs to your participants after the event. Post the best photographs on your bulletin boards, in the cafeteria or publish them in the company newsletter. Put them on your company's website so your teams' family members can view them from home.

If you record on video, have the footage edited with music and snappy graphics. Show this entertaining vignette another time at a company meeting or social event.

8. **Harness the power of peripheral players.**

When selecting participants for your program, be willing to include those related to, but not permanent members of, the core group. Internal customers, suppliers, and neighboring departments could all provide a few participants who are 'closely related' to your core group.

These 'peripheral players' can add significant value, perspective and insight to your program. They can also help with appropriate communication inside and outside your organization after the event is over.

9. **Get personal.**

Make sure everyone sees the link between 'group team building' and 'individual action' on the job. Have each person complete a commitment card, action plan, personal promise statement or some other means to ensure they apply appropriate new behaviors.

Closing a team building program by having everyone share their list of commitments and action plans is a good way to gain buy-in from individuals and unite the entire group.

10. **Reward the organizers.**

Planning and preparing a team building program is a major undertaking. Be sure to give recognition to those who did the work 'behind the scenes'. A thoughtful gift, given in front of everyone at the end of the program, will be appreciated and remembered.

Twelve tips to make your corporate conference more successful

Planning and conducting a successful corporate conference is an enormous and important task. Huge sums of money are usually invested. Huge amounts of time, too!

Here are twelve quick tips to help make your big event an even bigger success.

1. Use BIG, CLEAR names on nametags.

Use a bold, sans-serif typeface with the largest possible letter size. Nametags should be easy to read from at least 12 feet (3 meters) away. The whole purpose of a nametag is to make it easy for people to meet, mingle and say 'Hello!' No sense giving out nametags that require your conference participants to squint and stare.

2. Keep participants *hot* by keeping the room *cool*.

Keep your conference room temperature set toward cool. Studies show people are most alert at 62–64° Fahrenheit (16–17° Celsius).

Have participants move and stay active during the conference. If necessary, advise them in advance to wear a suit, light jacket or sweater.

This approach to room temperature is much better than looking out over an audience that is too warm, too cozy and too, too close to sleep!

3. Distribute a participants' networking sheet.

Gather names and complete contact information of all conference delegates. Assemble them in a user-friendly networking sheet for during and after your conference.

Use a digital camera to include head-and-shoulders portraits of each conference delegate. This makes it easy for participants to find each other during the event, and easier still to remember each other after the conference is over.

4. Use a variety of activities.

Keep your conference engaging and unique. Employ a wide range of conference activities: speeches; conference games; interactive workshops; exhibitions; panel discussions; question-and-answer sessions with presenters, customers and suppliers; themed meals; social events, etc.

5. Pick your theme and promote it.

Give your conference a distinctive theme and title. If your event is already known as 'The 3rd Annual Manufacturer's Convention' (or similar), then add a subtitle to the event to distinguish *this year's* event from the ones before and after.

Here are some examples of conference events I have helped design and conduct: 'Thriving in the Future', 'Riding the Waves of Change', 'New Opportunities, New Challenges', 'Putting Our Strategy to Work', 'Putting Our Customers on Top'.

When appropriate, couple your theme with an attractive logo to illustrates the key idea or message. Repeat the theme throughout your conference. Ask presenters to link their content and conclusions to your chosen theme, providing continuity and ongoing reinforcement.

Repeat the theme and/or logo on all your conference decorations and take-home material: folders, notebooks, nametags, banners, shirts, etc.

6. Set the look of conference presentations.

Once you decide on a theme and logo or illustration for your event, encourage presenters and exhibitors to use them in all their displays, take-home materials and presentation graphics.

Provide presenters and exhibitors with camera-ready images in hard copy, on CD, or by direct download from your website. Send these out early so there is plenty of time for everyone to customize their material, making *your* conference look good.

7. Begin before the conference.

Get your audience participating in the conference even *before* they arrive on-site. Send out advance mailings with selected readings, 'think-about' assignments, information-gathering responsibilities, a detailed program agenda, etc.

8. Continue the conference after it's over.

Extend and prolong conference value by sending out selected materials *after* the conference is over. Send a follow-up article, newsletter, results of a survey, printed version of action plans or decisions made during the conference, etc. Put your own cover letter on top of the package with thanks and congratulations to the delegates, and an invitation to your next conference event.

Put a page on your website with photographs from the conference, key ideas and articles presented at the event, survey results, etc. Promote the post-conference website during the conference itself.

9. Triple check all audio-visual equipment.

If the first thing your audience hears is 'Can you hear me in the back?', you have failed on this key point.

If the speaker says, 'Can we have the lights down please?' and the lights don't come down right away, you have failed on this key point.

To make your conference a success, *triple* check all microphones, projectors, screens, computers, music sources, lights, air-conditioning controls, etc.

And just in case, have back-ups ready to go if needed.

10. If you start with tea and coffee, schedule a 'bio-break' early.

Offering coffee and tea during conference registration is a very nice touch, especially if you include pastries and fresh fruit. But if your conference begins at 8:30 am, don't wait until 10:30 am to schedule the first break!

11. Begin with a bang.

Start your conference with a powerful video, captivating slides, stirring presentation, strong first speech, dramatic performance, multi-media extravaganza – or just about anything else that gets the audience interested and involved. When you start strong, your conference is off to a good start. When you start with a boring lecture from the CEO about last quarter's financial results, you will be trying to recover all day.

12. End with a memorable finale.

Make your final impression a lasting one. Close your conference with an amazing speaker, tear-jerking song, major award presentation, multi-media event or anything else that gets the audience motivated and reminds them why they came in the first place.

Twelve top tips for training an international audience

Training a worldwide audience can be a minefield of potential errors, missteps and disasters. Whether you have 30 or 300, it is likely that you will face men and women, old and young, company veterans and brand-new employees, locals and foreigners, married, single or recently divorced, and every possible mix of ethnic, religious and sexual persuasion. With a group like this, you can offend without intention, insult without meaning to, and alienate without even trying.

Avoid painful mistakes! Follow these twelve tips when you work with participants from around the world and you will find yourself with an attentive, involved and harmonious learning group.

1. Don't assume. Ask!

Don't assume everyone in the room is just like you or like anyone else! Acknowledge the diversity in the room. Highlight the rich range of life and business experience this group can represent.

Ask participants to share about themselves in small groups. Start with easy questions: business experience, educational background, places they have lived or worked. As conversation warms up, move to current business issues: ask their opinions on trends in the industry, entry of new competitors, products, technologies or government regulations. Then get right to the training topic at hand: have participants discuss expectations of the course, problems they need to solve, solutions they intend to discover.

Finally, when groups are well lubricated with rapport, ask participants to share about their personal lives – family, hobbies, vacations and other special interests.

2. **Speak very clearly and distinctly.**

Your native tongue may not be the first language of all your audience members. Adjust your presentation style so everyone can easily follow.

Years ago I spoke in Australia in front of a large international audience. Eleven countries were represented with seven different languages. Simultaneous translation was provided for non-native English speakers. Energized by the crowd, I launched into a presentation of humorous stories, anecdotes, case studies and key learning points. Throughout the speech, I was pleased to hear the Japanese contingent laughing at all of my jokes.

Or so it seemed. After the presentation, one Japanese participant set me straight: I was speaking so quickly, the interpreter was unable to keep up. Instead of translating my presentation, he gave up and spent most of the time talking in Japanese about how funny it was to see this American fellow rushing about in a big hurry on stage! I laughed when I heard this report, but I certainly learned the lesson: With an international audience, s-l-o-w d-o-w-n, and speak very clearly.

3. **Bridge the communication gap.**

Some of your group may be participating in a language that is not their native tongue. If their vocabulary or pronunciation is difficult for others to understand, you can bridge the gap by clearly repeating their comments and contributions.

Go beyond the spoken word to encourage understanding: use graphics, charts, pictures, video, physical examples, role-playing and other non-verbal techniques to get your points across.

4. Encourage everyone to participate.

Newcomers bring fresh perspective. Old-timers have experience and wisdom. Locals understand 'what's happening here and now'. Foreigners have a 'global' point of view.

Be liberal with your compliments and praise. 'That's a very good question!' let's everyone know it's safe to ask the next one. 'Thank you for your answer!' tells the whole room it's safe to venture a reply.

5. Be experienced, not exceptional.

Trainers are often widely experienced and well-traveled. They can bring good value to the group, but don't highlight the differences too much. You want respect, not distance. When connecting with an international group, a little humility goes a long way.

6. Speak the local language.

If possible, use local language, customs and examples in your presentation. This may require some preparation on your part, but it can make a very big impact on your group.

Toward the end of the Cold War, comedian Billy Crystal began a stand-up routine in Moscow by conducting the first five minutes entirely in Russian. But Billy Crystal doesn't speak Russian; he had memorized his entire opening act in translation! The Russian audience howled their approval and continued laughing as he delivered the rest of his show in English.

7. **Avoid phrases that do not translate well.**

   What is 'clear as a bell' to you may be 'thick as mud' in every other language. Avoid phrases that do not translate well. 'Six of one, half a dozen of the other', 'by the skin of your teeth', 'right as rain' and 'chicken with your head cut off' may translate nicely in your home town, but can bring real confusion and frustration overseas. Do you 'catch my drift'?

8. **If in doubt, leave it out.**

   Exercise great caution with your comments on politics, religion, sexuality, ethnic issues and humor. What is funny to one group may be downright offensive to another. There are plenty of things to laugh about in this world without poking fun at any one group. Make one mistake here and people could remember it forever.

9. **Triple check all translations.**

   If your presentation, workbook and handouts are translated into another language, check the choice of words and phrases many times. Use a professional translator who is familiar with your field of work. Then check it again with actual participants in your group.

   At the Service Quality Centre in Singapore, we use the phrase 'Never Settle' to mean 'strive for continuous improvement'. But when we first took this phrase overseas, it was translated into Mandarin like this: 'never agree in a negotiation'. And the phrase became 'don't sit down' in Indonesia!

10. **Mix up the group to increase participation.**

    Sharing experiences is one of the best aspects of international training. But don't count on participants to do it by themselves. Give the process a boost by mixing the group in various ways. Suppose you have 32 participants. You can combine them at various times into smaller teams of 2, 4, 6, 8 or even 16.

Do a random split by having them 'count off' with numbers around the room. Or have a bit more fun! I often divide my groups by date of birth, number of siblings, seniority with the company, first letter of their family name, length of hair, color of socks, you name it!

11. Assure talk time for all.

Some nationalities are naturally more outspoken than others. Be sure everyone gets a chance to speak up by structuring the sequence of participation. Once everyone is in small groups, have the most senior member of the group speak first, or the most junior. Ask the women to talk first, or those who have traveled from farthest away.

Acknowledge outspoken participants, but don't let them overwhelm the conversation. I often do this by having small groups nominate a spokesperson, then having that person nominate someone else in the group to speak on their behalf!

12. Bring them back together at the end.

Mixing everyone up is great for sharing new ideas. But be sure you bring everyone back together at the end to prioritize key points and generate new action steps. Have real work groups (whether by function, country, customer or project) explain the relevance of their learning to the job and state their plans for improvement and implementation.

Whether you have training to bring, a session to present or an important meeting to facilitate, these time-tested techniques will help bring out the best in your participants – and you!

What's the answer? Which tools and techniques do you prefer?

Answers in the Appendix...but who could you ask for help *before* turning the page?

Puzzle clues

Across

1   Motivating or inherent nature
4   Positive side effect
6   Consider carefully; reflect on
8   Select as an alternative
9   Clout or influence
11 Attitude of willingness to get the job done (hyph)
12 Distinctive; identify
13 Affinity between people
16 Show deference
17 Separate
18 Unyielding; grim
19 Just made
21 Spoil the appearance
23 Choice; choose
25 Curiosity; devotion
27 Actively smell (at)
28 Of lesser importance

Down

1   Speak quickly and angrily (at)
2   Irritate
3   Make something known
5   People we know and regard with affection and trust
6   A practical method applied reliably to a task
7   The knowledge and skill required to do something
8   Issued commands with authority
9   Reproduce from type
10 Succeeds
14 Always strive for a high ____ of customer care
15 Share your customers' feelings
20 Observe with attention
21 Slogan or saying
22 Depend (on)
24 Aim to make every customer feel at _____
26 CD___ (abbr.)

APPENDIX

CROSSWORD PUZZLE
ANSWERS AND
LEARNING RESOURCES

The puzzles in this book were created by
'Mr. Crossword' (Mr. Lakhi Sawlani).
You can write to him with clues of your own:
greatspeeches@yahoo.com

Puzzle this: How spectacular is your service?

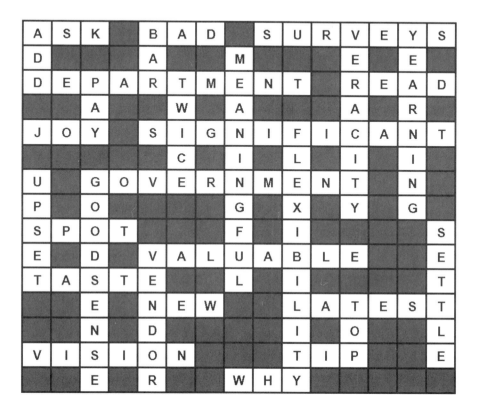

Answers for the puzzle in Chapter 1 on page 34.

How many did you solve before you turned to this page?

How many times will you assist a customer before you turn to a colleague and ask for help? Are you willing to keep trying? Are you willing to ask for help?

Test yourself: How can you add more value?

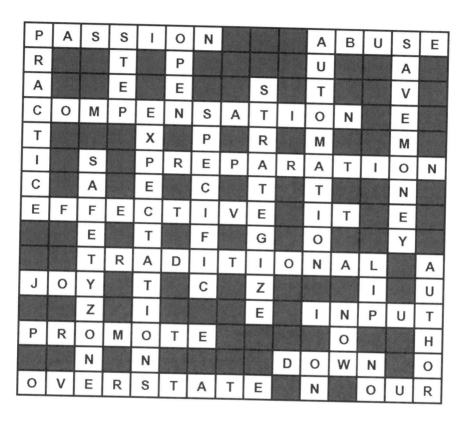

Answers for the puzzle in Chapter 2 on page 68.

Did you get them all? Does anyone have *all* the answers? Of course not. That's one more good reason to work with your colleagues in high-energy service *teams!*

Take the quiz: What are the little things that mean a lot?

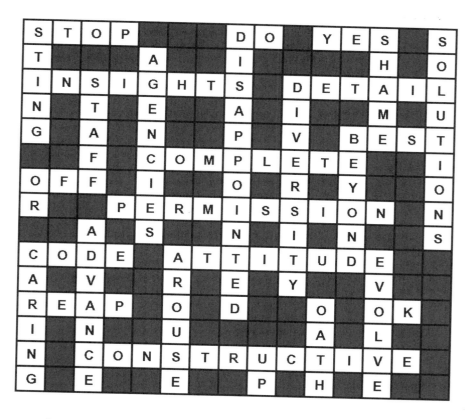

S	T	O	P			D	O			Y	E	S		S
T			A			I						H		O
I	N	S	I	G	H	T	S		D	E	T	A	I	L
N		T	E		A		I					M		U
G		A	N			P	V				B	E	S	T
		F	C	O	M	P	L	E	T	E				I
O	F	F		I			O	R	Y					O
R			P	E	R	M	I	S	S	I	O	N		N
		A	S			N		I		N				S
C	O	D	E		A	T	T	I	T	U	D	E		
A	V		R	E		Y					V			
R	E	A	P		O		D		O		O	K		
I		N		U			A			L				
N		C	O	N	S	T	R	U	C	T	I	V	E	
G		E		E		P		H		E				

Answers for the puzzle in Chapter 3 on page 92.

Which answers were easy? Which words took you longer? How well did you do?

Providing customer service is like that, too.

Some customers are easy to serve – no problem at all. Others may seem a real challenge at first (like a hard puzzle question). But challenging customers *can* be served well with your patience and focus (just like a good puzzle answer).

What do you think? Will you always go the extra mile?

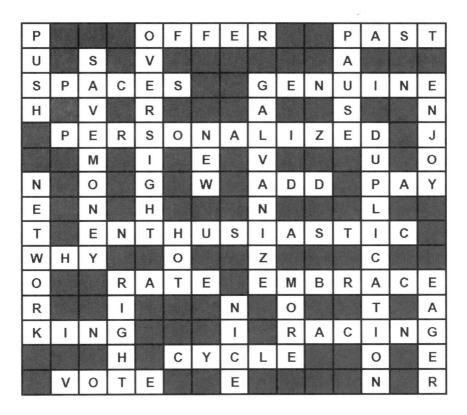

Answers for the puzzle in Chapter 4 on page 122.

Which clues had you simply stumped for answers?

Have you ever been in a service situation where you were stumped for the right thing to say or do?

When that happens, take a deep breath. Then kindly ask your customer for a moment to consult with your manager on the issue at hand. Then, like solving a difficult puzzle, you can work it out together.

Take this test and see: How much difference do you make?

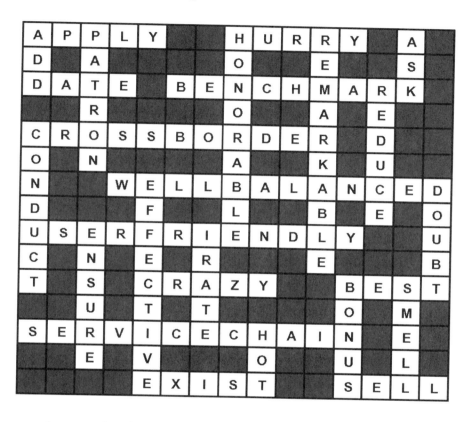

Answers for the puzzle in Chapter 5 on page 146.

Did you enjoy this puzzle? Which clue and answer did you enjoy the most?

Which customer service situations give you the greatest pleasure? Taking care of new customers, repeat customers, upset customers?

All of them are valuable – they're all *customers!*

Sharpen your pencil to build a beter service culture

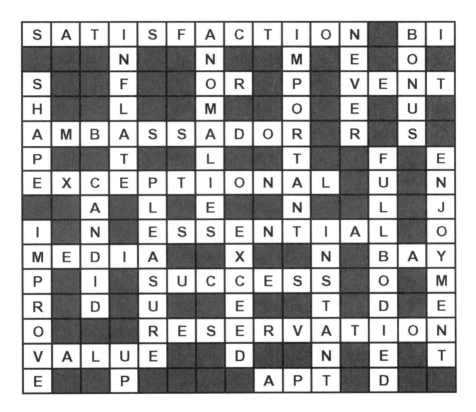

S	A	T	I	S	F	A	C	T	I	O	N		B	I
			N			N			M		E		O	
S			F			O	R		P		V	E	N	T
H			L			M			O		E		U	
A	M	B	A	S	S	A	D	O	R		R		S	
P			T			L			T			F		E
E	X	C	E	P	T	I	O	N	A	L		U		N
		A		L		E			N			L		J
I		N		E	S	S	E	N	T	I	A	L		O
M	E	D	I	A			X			N		B	A	Y
P		I		S	U	C	C	E	S	S		O		M
R		D		U			E			T		D		E
O				R	E	S	E	R	V	A	T	I	O	N
V	A	L	U	E			D			N		E		T
E			P					A	P	T		D		

Answers for the puzzle in Chapter 6 on page 180.

Did you make any mistakes? If so, that's good!

Making mistakes is *important* for a healthy and growing service culture. If no one ever tries anything new, you will have very few mistakes.

But what else happens if no one ever tries anything new?

Figure it out: Which point of view is right for you?

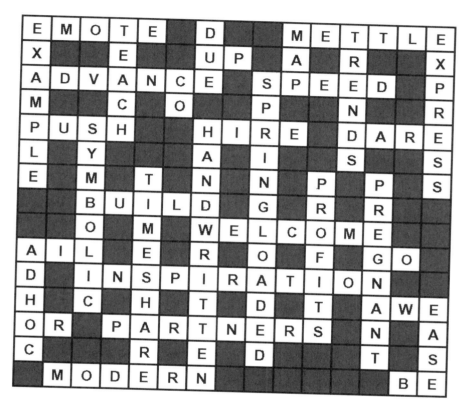

Answers for the puzzle in Chapter 7 on page 214.

What is *your* point of view when you think about service?

Is it something you do for a living? Or something to give because you *are* living?

Is service just for profits, markets and a competitive edge? Or is it a powerful way to increase the joy in your life and in the lives of others?

What's the answer? Which tools and techniques do you prefer?

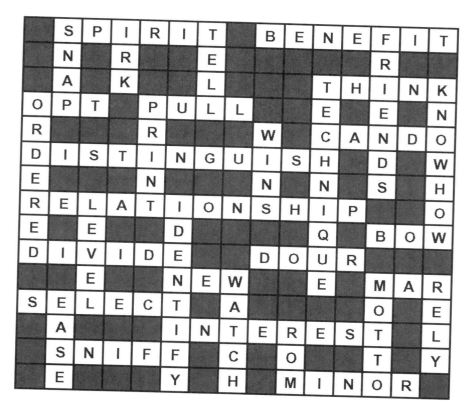

Answers for the puzzle in Chapter 8 on page 244.

Which service tools and techniques are well-polished in *your* collection?

Are you a great service provider over the counter, on the telephone, through e-mail, face-to-face?

Are you good with new customers who don't have a clue? Repeat customers who don't have much time?

UP Your Service! training programs

Everything you need in complete learning systems to get your service and your customers' loyalty going *UP!* Featuring Ron Kaufman in professionally produced video and audio. Easy-to-use and proven worldwide. *Backed by Ron's 100%, no-risk, money-back guarantee.* To order now, see page 267.

The Secrets of Superior Service™

Eight steps to achieve superior service:
- Fly over rising expectations
- Excellent service mindset
- Improving service standards
- Managing customer expectations
- Bounce back with service recovery
- Appreciate complaining customers
- Take personal responsibility
- See the world from your customer's point of view.

High-impact for frontline staff, supervisors and managers. Three hours on video and audio, including posters of key learning points, trainer's discussion guide and workbook.

S$388 (US$288) ISBN 981-00-8946-5

Partnership Power!™

How to build progressive and proactive partnerships inside and outside your organization. Best practices in the service cycle of *explore*, *agree*, *deliver* and *assure*.

Excellent for deepening relationships with your customers and suppliers, colleagues, distributors and other partners. These principles make sense in your personal life, too!

More than two hours on video and audio, plus complete viewer's guide with key learning points.

S$388 (US$288) ISBN 981-04-1787-X

Service Encounters of the Third Kind™

Shift your focus from simple 'transaction satisfaction' to creating profitable, long-term 'customer loyalty'. Discover the shifts you and your team must make in training, mindset, focus and goals.

Essential education for supervisors and management teams. The future is determined by the actions you take today. This shows you what to do! One hour on video and audio with viewer's guide.

S$288 (US$218) ISBN 981-00-8948-1

Quality Service - *LIVE!*

One of Ron's hottest presentations with a LIVE audience of 3,000 screaming fans. World-class education *and* motivation in a one-hour video that gets you pumped up and ready to *serve*. Terrific for team or staff meetings and fast training programs.

S$59 (US$39) ISBN 981-04-1661-X
Video in VCD format

Ron Kaufman is... *Unbelievable!*

Break through the glass ceiling to reach the very *top* and achieve your highest goals. Profit from this LIVE inspirational speech for an audience of 2,000 insurance agents in Singapore. Tailored for the industry and the local audience. One hour of fast-action ideas, insights and humor.

S$59 (US$39) ISBN 981-00-8949-X
Video in VCD format

• Achieve superior service
• Build strong partnerships
• Increase customer loyalty
ORDER NOW!

ACTIVE LEARNING RESOURCE	Amount	How Many?	Total
The Secrets of Superior Service™	s$388		
Partnership Power!™	s$388		
Service Encounters of the Third Kind™	s$288		
Quality Service - LIVE!	s$59		
Unbelievable!™	s$59		
UP Your Service!®	s$25		
UP Your Service INSIGHTS®	s$25		
UP Your Service GREAT IDEAS®	s$25		

All video programs are delivered in VCD format.
Fast Delivery: In Singapore by local courier – S$10.
International by air courier at cost.

Name :
Address :
Country : Code :
Telephone : Fax :
E-mail :
Credit Card Number :
VISA, MasterCard, American Express, Diners Club welcome.
Expiry date :
Signature:

Absolutely! UP Your Service right now!

1. Order **on-line** : www.RonKaufman.com/products.html
2. Order by **mail** : Ron Kaufman, 50 Bayshore Park #31-01 Aquamarine Tower, Singapore 914407
3. Order by **e-mail** : Ron@RonKaufman.com
4. Order by **fax** : (+65) 6444-8292

You — and your customers — will be delighted. Guaranteed!
Order these proven learning programs and enjoy them for ninety days. You will see improvemed service, happier customers and increased sales. Otherwise, simply return the package for a prompt and courteous refund.